A Christian Appeal to Reason
Here's what reviewers are saying . . .

"Let God be thanked for a book with a ringing affirmation that the living God of the Bible is at work in the world and that this God makes a difference. God made a difference for Abraham, Isaiah, and Paul. And he still makes a difference for the believer today. This is a Christian apologetic that refuses to treat the Christian faith merely academically but rather seeks 'to promote genuine faith in Christ.' This is a kind of apologetics that makes a difference!"

> —*Boyd Hunt*
> *Southwestern Journal of Theology*

"A very readable and practical book."

> —*The Church Herald*

"Ramm's exposition is orderly and lucid, and he strongly emphasizes scriptural data and principles in the defense of the faith."

> —Clifton Orlebeke
> *The Banner*

"Bernard Ramm, well known scholar and author, has made an outstanding contribution to the field of Christian Apologetics (the defense of the Christian Faith) in [*A Christian Appeal to Reason*]. The book is characterized by Ramm's clear and cogent reasoning. It is within the grasp of any person seriously pursuing the subject (which certainly is not true of some works in this field), and the Faith he defends is no irrational leap in the dark. Ramm wears well the mantle of great scholars of yesteryear, whom he quotes. His work would make an excellent text book for a College level class."

—J. D. Kennington
Conviction

"[*A Christian Appeal to Reason*] . . . will be a valuable tool for the Christian trying to give a reason for the hope that is in him. . . ."

—*Christianity Today*

"For a meaty, yet digestible, approach to the perennial questions of the proofs of God's existence and the problem of evil, see Bernard Ramm's latest in a long string of books on apologetics, [*A Christian Appeal to Reason*].

—*Interest*

A
Christian
Appeal
to
Reason

Bernard L. Ramm

WORD BOOKS
PUBLISHER
WACO, TEXAS

A Christian Appeal To Reason *by Bernard L. Ramm*

Originally published as The God Who Makes a Difference,
by Bernard L. Ramm

Copyright © 1972 by Word, Incorporated, Waco, Texas 76703

First Printing, June 1972
Second Printing, August 1974
First Paperback Printing, September 1977

Printed in the United States of America
ISBN 0-8499-2812-5
Library of Congress catalog card number: 70-188071

To all the students of Young Life Institute,
Fountain Valley, Colorado, who since 1955 and on
helped shape the form and contents of this book
by patiently listening to the development of the case
and responding in so many ways that in turn helped
the better development of my ideas

Contents

Preface

Not all of my opinions on Christian apologetics are in this book. My first venture into the field was in 1948 in a little volume now out of print titled *Problems in Christian Apologetics*. The value of that book lies not in what it taught other people but in what I learned from writing it. Eventually, through the correspondence from that book and later from the writings of those men, I became much indebted at certain key points to E. J. Carnell and Gordon Clark.

My second adventure into this field was a book called *Types of Apologetic Systems*. That too is out of print, but another version of it, *Varieties of Christian Apologetics*, is at the time of this writing still in print. It is a study of the apologetic position of nine different men.

Next I tried to restate the case for Christian evidences in the light of the latest in theology, science, and philosophy. I tried to preserve what was good in the older works and restate the case for evidences for the twentieth century. I modified certain lacks of the book in an article, "The Evidence in Prophecy and Miracle" in *Revelation and the Bible* which was edited by Carl Henry. The title of the book was *Protestant Christian Evidences*.

Feeling that the evangelical cause was being led down the wrong street with reference to science, I published *The Christian View of Science and Scripture* (1954). It also appeared in a British edition.

Other works that relate somewhat to Christian apologetics are: *The Pattern of Religious Authority, Special Revelation and the Word of God*, and *The Witness of the Spirit*. The last book is very important for Christian apologetics and theoretically should be incorporated as a whole within this book, but its main elements only will be utilized.

The intention of this book is that it will serve primarily as a textbook. It is true that I set forth my own position in Christian apologetics and do not merely list opinions and options. But the book is written as a point of departure for use in the classroom as the instructor so wishes.

Not every important topic of Christian apologetics can be discussed

11

here. We have therefore limited the scope of our work to three essential parts: (1) our own basic theory; (2) the great positive achievement of theism, the existence of God; and (3) the great negative threat to theism, the problem of evil. The final chapter is a series of problems that may be developed in a number of ways so that the instructor may shape the course as he wishes.

There is one point that needs some clarification. Barth does not teach an express apologetics, but in reality he has a very significant one. His massive doctrine of revelation in *Church Dogmatics* I/1 and I/2 and his doctrine of the reality of God in II/1 are really apologetic treatises of the first order, and some of that material has filtered into these pages.

I
The Nature and Function
of Christian Apologetics

Section 1: The Threefold Task of Apologetics

Because the expression *Christian apologetics* is almost universally misunderstood, there can be no discussion of the topic until it is explained.

In the Greek language the basic meaning of the verb *to apologize* means to defend oneself in a court of law. The defense that was made was called an *apology*. The most famous instance of this in history is the case of Socrates. He was charged with being an atheist (one who did not believe in the gods accepted by the state) and a corrupter of the youths of Athens. He gave his great speech before the Athenian court of law. We have no writings of Socrates himself. What we know of him comes basically through the famous *Dialogues of Plato*.[1] The dialogue that gives us Socrates' speech of defense is simply called "Apology."

Both the verb *to make an apology* and the noun *apology* occur in the New Testament Greek text, but the English translation obscures this. In the attempt to give the text a smoother English character, the translators used such expressions as *to give answer, to make one's defense*, or simply *defense*. Apologetics is then a New Testament word and a New Testament activity. In simplest definition Christian apologetics is the defense of the Christian faith.

For example, Peter wrote: "Always be prepared to make a defense

---

1. Plato, *Dialogues*, 4th ed., trans. Benjamin Jowett (New York: Oxford University Press, 1953).

[Greek, *apologia*] to any one who calls you to account for the hope that is in you" (1 Pet. 3:15, RSV).

Paul wrote: "We live in the flesh, of course, but the muscles that we fight with are not flesh. Our war is not fought with weapons of flesh, yet are strong enough, in God's cause, to demolish fortresses. We demolish sophistries, and the arrogance that tries to resist the knowledge of God; every thought is our prisoner, captured to be brought into obedience to Christ" (2 Cor. 10:3-6, JB). A better definition of the character and function of Christian apologetics would be hard to give than these words of Paul.

As the Christian church spread into the Roman Empire, it was resisted by the philosophers and intellectuals. Christianity was judged an absurd religion. In reply to these philosophers and intellectuals there arose a group of men known as the Second Century Apologists, or simply as the Apologists (Aristides, Justin Martyr, Tatian, Athenagoras, Theophilus, Minucius Felix, and Tertullian).

These writings contained many different elements. They were primarily defenses of the Christian faith attempting to remove the various kinds of accusations made against it. But they did contain some positive materials, by which we mean arguments or reasons which supported the truthfulness of Christian belief. Eventually the transition took place in which it became apparent that the main burden of Christian apologetics was to set forth the positive grounds for Christian faith, not to answer accusations. This does not mean that apologies or defenses of the Christian faith ceased to exist. Christian apologetics as the reply to the critics of Christianity is an activity that pervades the whole history of Christian thought even until the present time in which books of this nature are still being written. However, if any one man can be picked out as setting Christian apologetics permanently in the new direction of positive affirmation rather than critical reply, it would be Augustine. In such books as *On True Religion*, the *City of God*, and the *Confessions*, he gives the positive reasons for believing Christianity to be true. However, apologetic materials are to be found in many of Augustine's works, and the three books mentioned are only examples and do not constitute the whole body of Augustine's thoughts on Christian apologetics.

No uniform phrase has been adopted to express the idea of Christian apologetics. Unfortunately many great books written on Christian apologetics have not been suspected as such because their unfortunate titles did not indicate their contents. Nor have the Christian apologists agreed on any uniform method in developing Christian apologetics. Two books have appeared recently on the history of apologetics, but they are so sketchy that they betray as much as they explain.[2]

Our immediate concern is to set out what we think the function of Christian apologetics is for our century in the light of its historical development and in perspective of modern learning. The *first* function of Christian apologetics is to show how the Christian faith is related to truth claims.

All of the great religions perform several functions. One of these functions is to determine how God is to be worshiped and what kind of liturgy, rites, or ceremonies concretely express this worship. Most religions teach the value of personal devotions such as prayer, meditation, or reading the book of the religion. Religions also express themselves theologically whenever they set forth what they believe or describe their central tenets.

When a religion becomes acutely self-conscious, it sees and feels the need of facing the problem of truth. The practices of any given religion are valid only if the supporting system or theses behind these practices are true.

Frequently religion is expressed as a matter of faith. This usually means that religion is a personal matter. It expresses one's feelings about the universe as a whole or the significance of human life or the worthiness of certain ethical convictions. In this context, religion presumes to be outside the territory of truth claims, for the very way faith is understood means that it is not concerned with testable materials.

Such a view of religion is superficial. All human disciplines must come to terms with truth, and the magnitude of the claims of at least the great historical religions demands that religion too come to terms with the problem of truth. A religion that does not conform to reality, however reality is defined at the moment, is a fiction. Perhaps it would be more accurate to say that it is an accretion of fictions acquired through the centuries. A religion cannot rest upon fiction or fictions but must be anchored in reality. Only as we examine truth claims about a religion can we know the relationship of the religion to reality.

Religion cannot rest on presumptive grounds or a traditional heritage. If it has not brought to the surface in a conscious and self-critical way

---

2. J. K. S. Reid, *Christian Apologetics* (Grand Rapids: William B. Eerdmans, 1969) ; Avery Dulles, *A History of Apologetics* (New York: Corpus Books, 1971).

the question of truth, it is a religion yet in its infancy. No tradition, no matter how long and no matter how highly honored, can be considered true solely on the grounds of its long standing.

In harmony with the ancient concept of apologetics as one's legal defense before a court of law, Christian apologetics too is such an activity. It is the conscious, deliberate defense and vindication of Christian theology as truth. It is deliberately interacting with the critical criteria of truth in order to show that the realities of which the Christian faith speaks are indeed true realities.

Because Christian apologetics interacts with truth claims, it contains much philosophical material. This is necessary. Those men of our culture whose expert learning is in the nature of logic and theories of truth are the philosophers. Any kind of support of a religious system involves some kind of proof. The theologian is not obligated to take the word of any given philosopher about truth claims, but he must interact with truth claims as discussed, analyzed, and evaluated by the philosophers. Any claim for the truth of a religion appeals to some criterion or criteria, but any criterion appealed to has already been the subject of discussion among philosophers. Christian apologetics cannot avoid then much concern with philosophical materials.

This is not to turn the Christian faith over to philosophy as if to subject its divine origin to a human judgment, or its uniqueness to man's curiosity, or its authenticity to unregenerate men. If Christian apologetics is concerned with truth, it must interact with truth claims. Theories of truth are part of the technical study of philosophy. The Christian apologist is forced to enter the field of philosophy if he is to face the question of truth in genuine integrity of both spirit and methodology.

Unfortunately, in the history of philosophy many theories of truth have been set forth and defended so there is no one theory of truth. Further, different subject matters require tests for truth that are unique to that subject matter, so in some instances it is the subject matter that dictates what kind of theory of truth will be employed. And yet that is not enough. Some of these theories of truth are very sophisticated and would require pages and pages of exposition to make them meaningful to the average reader. Plato's logic is dialectical, but it is very difficult to explain to a person with no background in philosophy or logic what Plato meant by dialectical.

A mystic may argue that his experience is so real, so self-authenticating, so vivid, so given of God, that it is impossible to doubt it. In fact if he doubted it, he would have to question his sanity. The very force or intensity or quality of the experience convinces the person that he is experiencing the truth.

Or, a person may say that a proposition is true because it agrees with, or coheres with, everything else that he knows. It does not contradict any other proposition that the person accepts. This is easiest to illustrate in mathematics. The mathematical theorem that seven plus five is twelve is true because it is consistent with the axioms (basic assumptions) of mathematics and does not conflict with any other theorem in mathematics.

Or, a person may say that a proposition is true because it agrees with the facts. The proposition that wax is a soft material at room temperature can be readily verified with the blade of a pocket knife. That a green apple is sour can be tested by a bite into one. Of course, when we move on to theories in science, we need tests more sophisticated than scratching with a knife or biting into an apple, but the idea is the same. The facts support the proposition.

Again it may be argued that propositions are not true or false in terms of some eternal logic or abstract theory of truth. If we can do something about a proposition, the proposition is a meaningful one; if we can't, it is a meaningless one. If we claim that heat melts lead, we can set up an experiment and see what happens. If there is nothing that we can do about a proposition (such as "planets are pushed by invisible angels"), then the proposition is meaningless.

This is but a popular presentation of some of the tests for truth. A thorough discussion of the theories of truth would require an entire volume. As the argument in this book moves along, we will delve deeper and deeper into the problem of truth and see how logic and truth function in Christian apologetics. That will come naturally with the exposition of materials so no comprehensive discussion of theory of truth is necessary at this point.

The only point we are trying to make here is that every apologist uses some kind of theory of truth or some kind of logical support for his beliefs. He may not be aware that he is doing this, but nevertheless he is. The only justifiable procedure for the Christian apologist is to show that he recognizes this problem and is articulate about the kind of theory of truth he uses or what kind of appeals to logic he makes.

The *second* function of Christian apologetics is to show Christianity's power of interpretation. If Christianity is true, it then has powers of interpretation that go with its being true.

Theories are held to be true not only from strictly logical reasons or empirical data but also because of their power to illuminate their subject matter or, as stated above, because of their power to interpret given topics or areas of subject matters.

A man believes in Marxism not only because he accepts the theoretical foundations of Marxism but because he believes the Marxian interpretation of history makes more sense than any alternative view. A Freudian not only knows his Freudian literature but he believes that the Freudian overall view of human nature is richer with insights and powers of interpretation than any other competitive psychology. Einstein's theories do have specific verification, but the physicist "feels at home" as he works with Einstein presuppositions in his daily work in the laboratory.

The principle of verification works in reverse (that is, falsification). A medical doctor rejects other theories of the pathology of disease because as a whole they seem out of joint. Or a physiologist may reject some food fad because it runs counter to all that he knows about dietetics. Theories may then be accepted because of the comfortable feel they give the scientist as he works with them or rejected because they seem at odds and ends with his general understanding of his subject matter.

The goal of Christian apologetics is also to show the interpretative power of the Christian faith in a variety of subjects. The Christian believes that his doctrine of man throws more light on the total understanding of man than any other philosophy or psychology. He believes that the Christian doctrine of sin gives the best of perspectives in understanding man's evil, depravities, and cruelties than any alternate theory of human cupidity. He believes that the doctrine of the Incarnation gives man the largest possible framework within which he may think of God, the knowledge of God, and the processes of revelation and redemption. He believes that the ethical insights of Holy Scripture enable him to think about ethical problems with more penetration, insight, and ideas for solutions than competing philosophical ethics.

The *third* function of Christian apologetics is that of refutation. It contains within itself the concept of apology, the defense of Christianity against false or spurious attacks.

From the moment the Christian gospel was first preached in the Book of Acts ("They are filled with new wine," Acts 2:13, RSV) until the present hour, the Christian faith has been accused of many things. The Jews have always considered Christianity as apostasy from Moses. The philosophers of the Greco-Roman world charged Christianity with being foolish. The Muslims in the Middle Ages thought the doctrines of Incarnation and Trinity irrational. Hume and Kant attempted to show that the theoretical or philosophical foundations of Christian theology were not capable of sustaining themselves in the face of modern analysis. The appeal to biblical miracles and fulfilled prophecy as divine seals of Christian revelation were rejected on scientific, historical, critical, theological, and philosophical grounds. Analytic or linguistic philosophy does not consider statements of Christian theology to be true or false but senseless or meaningless. Any proposition that cannot be tested is meaningless, and the affirmations of Christian theology cannot be tested so they are meaningless—not true or false. Sartre rejects the Christian doctrine of God, for in his opinion any external force or pressure corrupts the existential authenticity of man—God included! Many modern psychiatrists believe that what they discover in counseling about love, sexuality, marriage, and morality runs counter to Christian teaching.

To answer all of these objections is out of the question. The Christian apologists must select those objections he thinks most serious.

It might be of some help to notice some of the older objections to Christianity. Muslims and Jews frequently charged that the Christian doctrine of the Trinity was in matter of fact polytheism no matter how carefully the Creed of Athanasius ruled out this interpretation. Romans accused the Christians of cannibalism because they misunderstood the Lord's Supper. The odd meeting times of the early Christians were thought to be sessions for immorality rather than an attempt to evade persecution. Many of the attacks on Christianity have been based on philosophies which are now considered dated. For example, Hume cannot have it both ways. He cannot deny the existence of miracles in the manner in which he treats causation and at the same time maintain his "causeless" philosophy.

Section 2: Preliminary Considerations of Christian Apologetics

The practical value of apologetics. Christian apologetics does work on a theoretical level. It operates within various theological and philosophical concepts, but it is not a purely academic or theoretical activity. It not only attempts to establish the basis upon which Christianity is held as true, but it has certain practical benefits.

First, whenever a Christian speaks, whether he is part of a small group or a Bible study, or whether he is preaching a sermon, he speaks as a person. The more complete a person is, the more he speaks with integrity. In apologetics the Christian exposes himself to the critical problem of truth, to the challenges from atheism, agnosticism, and any other form of unbelief. He has to struggle, to think, to read, to criticize, to sift to see how it is with the Christian faith. He has to face the temptation of doubt and the feeling of uncertainty. When the Christian goes through this kind of an experience, knows the real objections to his faith, knows some significant answers to these objections, and knows the positive grounds for Christian assertions, he is a better person. Being a better person he then communicates his faith with greater integrity.

Second, having studied the various reasons for believing that Christianity is true, he now knows what he may or may not use in his public presentations. For example, he learns the difference between persuading people and manipulating people. He learns the limits of any argument based on experience. He knows what kind of arguments for the Christian faith have become obsolete or must be seriously qualified. Older books on Christian evidences spoke of the great benefit of the Christian church to man's progress as part of the case for Christianity. Any critically informed historian is aware of the sordid things done by the church in the name of Christ and Christianity such as religious wars, the Spanish Inquisition, the Crusades, and the Massacre of St. Bartholomew's Day.

Furthermore, the Christian will appeal to those kinds of arguments that are ethically sound, rationally correct, and grounded in the best possible interpretation of Scripture (if that is part of the argument). If he can do this, he anchors the faith of the convert with the right kind of arguments. Christian workers are always apprehensive that in the future the faith of their convert will be undermined. If the convert has been given some very shoddy arguments for the truth of the Christian faith, he becomes an easy victim of a critical refutation of such arguments. Converts may develop doubt, skepticism, and agnosticism if their faith is grounded upon insecure reasons, especially when these insecure or inadequate or shoddy arguments are exposed by competent scholars.

Third, in Christian work there is always the possibility of encountering objections to the Christian faith. Christians with some understanding of Christian apologetics are not at a complete loss when this situation arises. They have some idea of a point of departure or some idea of problems and answers.

Attitudes of theologians toward Christian apologetics. There is no standard Christian apologetics among Protestants. Roman Catholic scholars are expected to work within the general framework of the writings of Thomas Aquinas (although in recent Catholic thought there are some evasive tactics among the theologians to avoid being bound to a philosophy of the Middle Ages). Because there is no standard or normative view of Christian apologetics among Protestants in particular, the function of Christian apologetics differs from theologian to theologian.

Some theologians believe that Christianity can be demonstrated as true. The function of apologetics is to supply the church with a demonstration of the truthfulness of its philosophy. If Saint Thomas used the word *demonstration* as we use it, then he proposed to demonstrate that Christianity is true.

Some apologists think that Christian evidences demonstrate Christianity is true (in contrast to Saint Thomas's philosophical arguments). If a man rejects Christianity, there is nothing wrong with the Christian revelation. The man who rejects Christianity is perverse or motivated by ill will or does not grasp the cogency of the arguments.

Some theologians believe that the function of apologetics is to show the unique kind of verification required for the proof of a divine revelation. Apologetics is for the service of Christians and only indirectly for non-Christians. Christianity is to be verified by criteria which correspond to the nature of Christianity, and to impose upon Christianity criteria of truthfulness foreign to the nature of the Christian faith is to do it a grave injustice.

Certainly all apologists wish to show that Christianity is not verified by an appeal to a special kind of explainable psychological mechanism, to some type of argument which a capable logician would have no time shredding, or to a factual basis that a scientist or a historian could readily wash away.

Although Emil Brunner has a very neatly articulated apologetics in his work *Revelation and Reason*, he prefers the word *eristics*, derived from the Greek word meaning "to debate, to strive." To him the main emphasis of apologetics falls on the refutation of spurious attacks upon Christianity. The contention running through his book is that non-Christians misunderstand the essence of Christianity and so reject it on false grounds. However, his book *Truth as Encounter* (second edition) is an existentialist apologetics for the Christian faith. By eristics Brunner seeks to remove unnecessary obstacles to faith; by his Kierkegaardian existentialism he wishes to show the positive grounds of Christian faith which certainly are unique as Brunner sets them up.

Those theologians in the analytic or linguistic tradition apparently conceive of apologetics as showing how theological sentences assert, that is, how they are in some sense real propositions. Out of a wealth of litera-ture I can mention only Ian T. Ramsey, *Religious Language*,[3] and his American admirer, Jerry Gill, *The Possibility of Religious Language;*[4] Ronald Santoni, editor, *Religious Language and the Problem of Reli-gious Knowledge;*[5] and Dallas High, editor, *New Essays on Religious Language.*[6]

Some theologians believe that there is no such discipline as Christian apologetics. To some the experience of Jesus Christ is so real and trans-forming that any rational attempt to shore it up would be blasphemy against the Holy Ghost. The usual terms for this are Pietism and Fideism (*fide*, Latin, faith, hence awkwardly, *faithism*).

Barth is also in this camp to the degree that at least on the surface he professes to have nothing to do with apologetics. Apologetics presumes a stance outside of the Christian faith from which the apologist attempts to show the veracity of the Christian faith. To Barth this is a serious mistake. It presumes that a sinful man can test the revelation of an infinite, holy, and mysterious God. It puts the Lord on the carpet before the servant. It depreciates the ability of the divine revelation to carry its own credentials and establish its own beachhead.

But this is very much a paper attack. Barth's doctrine of revelation, his doctrine of the work of the Spirit in the reception of revelation, his doctrine of signs of revelation, and his doctrine of the reality of God are all important apologetical materials. It bleeds through every volume of the massive *Church Dogmatics* that if a man could see the entire scope of Christian theology in all its greatness he could not help but confess its truthfulness and become a believer. Barth's exhaustive *Church Dog-matics* is his Christian apologetics.

Rudolph Bultmann espouses a unique existentialistic apologetics. Faith and knowledge are as antithetical as one can find in the history of theology. Faith in the kerygma or in the encounter with God along with its manifold blessings is self-validating. Faith is decision, and an existen-tial decision of faith cannot be shored up by historical proofs, Christian evidences, or any other kind of support, or else it would lose its *qualia* as faith. Matters of fact are settled by the methodologies of matters of fact. Faith expresses itself in decision—decision for the kerygma. One of

---

3. London: SCM Press, 1957.

4. Grand Rapids: Wm. B. Eerdmans, 1971.

5. Bloomington: Indiana University Press, 1968.

6. New York: Oxford University Press, 1969.

the reasons Bultmann is against any new quests for the historical Jesus is that the expressed or unexpressed thesis is that the more we know of the historical Jesus the more secure our faith will be.

The relationship of philosophy to Christian faith. In certain passages Paul seems to place a veto on philosophy. Divine revelation is set over against human wisdom in such a way that the two seem incompatible.

"See to it that no one makes a prey of you by philosophy and empty deceit" (Col. 2:8, RSV).

"Has not God made foolish the wisdom of the world?" (1 Cor. 1:20, RSV). First Corinthians 1:17–31 is a diatribe against human wisdom and the character of human reasoning. Verse 20 is given as a sample for the entire passage.

"And my speech and my message were not in plausible words of wisdom" (1 Cor. 2:4, RSV).

"The unspiritual man does not receive the gifts of the Spirit of God, for they are folly to him, and he is not able to understand them because they are spiritually discerned" (1 Cor. 2:14, RSV).

"For the mind that is set on the flesh is hostile to God; it does not submit to God's Law, indeed it cannot; and those who are in the flesh cannot please God" (Rom. 8:7–8, RSV).

The word *philosophia* literally means "the love of wisdom." Historically philosophers were a class of men interested in knowledge for the sake of knowledge and not for any kind of monetary gain. They were motivated by love, *philia*, not by silver and gold. Nothing is wrong then in philosophy as such, and furthermore one cannot assume that the word *philosophy* in Colossians 2:8 is the same thing referred to as philosophy in the catalog of a university. Although some Christians have made this identification, there is no such one-to-one relationship.

Paul uses the word *philosophy* to mean any system which competes with divine revelation. In the same sense he challenges the wise man (Greek, *sophos*, possibly a philosopher), the scribe (the expert on religious matters), and the debater *of this age* (1 Cor. 1:20, italics mine). In writing Colossians, Paul was evidently referring to one of the religious cults of that day and not to our academic discipline of philosophy, and he rejected it on solid grounds. However, the ultimate grounds upon which it was rejected must be carefully determined. It was rejected because it was a human project. Paul does not reject this philosophy by making a careful analysis of its errors or mistakes or internal contradictions. He rejects it for the level on which it operates—the human level. As a human schema it cannot compete with the schema of divine revelation. Wherever philosophy is understood as purely a human conjecture and in competition with the revelation of the truth of God in Jesus Christ, Paul vetoes it.

Since modern philosophy is composed of many different subjects, it cannot be assessed in one uniform lump.

In some instances philosophers do create systems like materialism or pantheism or idealism or pragmatism. At this point the possibility of conflict between Christianity and philosophy is the greatest, and this is where Paul's veto would be more likely to apply.

But philosophers study many other topics such as logic, theory of art, philosophy of science, and philosophy of history. Certainly the Scriptures continuously use one form or another of logical argumentation— the argument from analogy, the argument from the law of noncontradiction, or the argument from the greater to the lesser. All argumentation for a particular Christian doctrine or a particular Christian theology is based on one or more of the very arguments found in a book of philosophical logic. If a Christian rules out all philosophy, he must rule out all Scripture passages that utilize some typical form of philosophical reasoning. And no theology could be written, no particular doctrine defended without recourse to some kind of logical method or form found in any elementary text on logic. To rule out all philosophy as anti-Christian is to rule out too much; in fact, it would make theology an impossibility.

Furthermore, philosophy deals with specialized studies such as ethical theory, philosophy of history, philosophy of science, political philosophy, and aesthetics (philosophy of the beautiful). Although the Christian theologian need not agree with any one particular school within these studies, the very knowledge of these studies gives him the kind of broad background necessary for apologetics. For example, the backbone of Holy Scripture is the historical thread that runs from Genesis to Revelation. The theologian needs to know philosophy of history to be able to give a competent evaluation of the form of biblical history. Furthermore, commencing with Augustine's *City of God*, many Christians have written philosophies of history. These philosophies of history have in common a strong apologetic motivation. Therefore, the theologian must know philosophy of history to evaluate competently the different Christian philosophies of history.

There are other very specific services of philosophy to theology and apologetics. Certain *topics* are discussed by both philosophers and theologians. The existence of God, the human soul, and the problem of evil have a long philosophical history. An apologist certainly increases his competence when he knows the philosophical studies which parallel his theological studies.[7]

Certain *objections* to Christianity spring directly from the philosophy of the objector. If the apologist knows the particular philosophy, he can assert that the criticism is really from philosophical prejudice and not from the character of Christianity itself. Or, he can show the failings of the particular philosophy and that therefore its criticisms of Christianity are invalid.

The philosopher Hume, one of the greatest of the philosophic critics of the Christian faith, defended a very radical and skeptical empiricism. Kant attacked the traditional doctrines of God and man on the basis of a critical idealism. In this century the British philosopher Ayer attempted to show that theology was meaningless from the standpoint of analytic philosophy or linguistic analysis philosophy. The apologist who knows the philosophies of these men knows on what basis they criticize the Christian faith and can assess the validity of such a criticism. He may attempt to refute particular theses of these objectors or else criticize the entire philosophy and in this way undermine the objections.

Certain philosophies and religions *compete* with Christianity. The only adequate way of negating such competition is for the Christian apologist to know rather thoroughly the presuppositions of the philosophy and the philosophical background of the religion. Otherwise his refutation will be superficial at best.

Many of the great *apologists of the past* consciously used a prevailing philosophy of the day. If the contemporary apologist wishes to know the history of apologetics, he must have adequate philosophical background to understand the philosophies that influenced such historical apologetical systems. Augustine was influenced by Plato and neo-Platonism; Thomas leaned heavily on Aristotle; Butler was a student of Locke; and Brunner was a disciple of Kierkegaard. The interactions and overlappings of philosophy with Christian apologetics is so great that no person can really dare to enter the area of Christian apologetics in a competent way without some mastery of the history of philosophy.

Another aspect of the problem of Christianity and philosophy is the claim that the New Testament is infiltrated by philosophies prevailing

---

7. A famous book for the study of philosophical topics that is of great value to the Christian apologist is J. Janet and G. Séailles, *A History of the Problems of Philosophy*, 2 vols. (New York: Macmillan, 1902).

at the time it was written. Some have felt that Paul was significantly influenced by Stoic philosophy (from *stoa*, "a collonade where Stoicism was taught"; Stoicism was founded by Zeno of Citium, 335–263 B.C.). This philosophy teaches a strong doctrine of natural law and law of conscience which seems to have parallels in Paul's writings. Edwin Hatch (1835–89) wrote a famous book *The Influence of Greek Ideas on Christianity*[8] in which he maintained that much early Christian writing and many Christian creeds were influenced by Greek ideology. This idea was picked up by Adolph Harnack (1851–1930), the greatest church historian of his time, and given a wide hearing. To this day it is one of the unsifted presuppositions of modern theological scholarship that early Christian thought was corrupted by Greek substance philosophy.

Bultmann has defended the thesis that huge sections of the New Testament are cast in the mythological thought forms and imageries of the ancient world. In modern times it is also thought that Paul made concessions to, or revealed influence from, Greek philosophy in his Acts 17 speech.[9]

Christian apologists have exhibited many different attitudes toward philosophy. A glance at three of these (the most widely accepted) will give some preliminary perspective on the problem of the relationship of Christian faith to philosophy.

To some, philosophy is the work of unregenerate man or the product of demons or perhaps even the work of Satan himself. This being the case the Christian theologian must have nothing to do with philosophy. From this perspective, philosophy will always be in direct competition to Christian revelation and a permanent, vicious enemy of Christian theology.

To some, philosophy anticipates or parallels Christian theology. At some time or other Plato, Aristotle, Plotinus, Hegel, Bowne, and Heidegger have been counted as real allies in the defense of Christian theology. That a philosophy should be found to be in perfect or near perfect accord with Christian theology has been taken to indicate the philosophical validation of the Christian faith. Thus Hegel's statement that theology put in symbolic form what philosophy taught in literal language was taken to indicate the supreme philosophical verification of Christianity.

---

8. Magnolia. Mass.: Peter Smith, 1958.

9. Cf. Bertil Gärtner, *The Areopagus Speech and Natural Revelation* (London: C. W. K. Gleerup, 1955).

Others have thought that philosophy offers a tool, a number of instruments, a kind of guide for the writing of Christian theology and apologetics. No one philosophy is adhered to, but all philosophies are considered. Hence, philosophy has an instrumental service in theology but not a magisterial service. Of the three positions, this one is most capable of defense.

This latter point needs some short comment in relation to Luther's attitude toward philosophy and reason. Luther's statements that castigate Aristotle, reason, and philosophy are meant to show the real difference between products of human reasoning and products of divine revelation. But where reason is in the service of Christian theology, it is one of God's choicest gifts and shows the infinite difference the Creator has made between man and beast. In fact, Calvin's position is not too much different. The philosophical elements found in Luther (such as ideas from Occam or Biel) and Calvin (Platonism, Stoicism) simply indicate an inability to follow through a program consistently. This factor makes it obvious that as long as we are sinners our theology will always have foreign philosophical elements in it.

BIBLIOGRAPHY

General reference works in which men or topics are discussed:

Brunotte, Heinz, and Weber, Otto. *Evangelisches Kirchen Lexikon.* 4 vols. Göttingen: Vanhenhoeck and Ruprecht, 1961.

Cross, F. L., ed. *Oxford Dictionary of the Christian Church.* New York: Oxford University Press, 1958.

Edwards, Paul, ed. *Encyclopedia of Philosophy.* 8 vols. New York: Macmillan, 1967.

Galling, Kurt, ed. *Die Religion in Geschichte und Gegenwart,* 5 vols. 3d ed. Tübingen: J. C. B. Mohr, 1957.

Hastings, J., ed. *Encyclopedia of Religion and Ethics.* 13 vols. New York: Charles Scribner's Sons, 1928.

Kittel, G., and Friedrich, G., eds. *Theological Dictionary of the New Testament.* 7 vols. Grand Rapids: Eerdmans, 1964, 1965, 1966–69.

Runes, D. D., ed. *Dictionary of Philosophy.* Totowa, N.J.: Littlefield, 1960.

Ziegenfuss, Werner, ed. *Philosophen Lexikon.* 2 vols. Berlin: Walter de Gruyter, 1949.

Helpful materials will be found in all histories of philosophy, all histories of theology, all works on patrology, all works on the history of the philosophy of religion.

Since philosophy of religion, philosophical theology, Christian philosophy, and apologetics overlap, the bibliographical references will reflect this.

Brightman, E. *A Philosophy of Religion.* New York: Prentice-Hall, 1949. Page 490 and on contains a historical bibliography of the great works in philosophy of religion followed by a general bibliography.

Casserly, J. V. Langmead. *The Christian in Philosophy.* New York: Charles Scribner's Sons, 1951. Part 1 is historical survey.

Collins, James D. *The Emergence of Philosophy of Religion.* New Haven, Conn.: Yale University Press, 1967. Centers in Hume, Kant, and Hegel.

Dulles, Avery. *A History of Christian Apologetics.* New York: Corpus Books, 1971.

Farrar, A. S. *A Critical History of Free Thought in Reference to the Christian Religion.* London: John Murray, 1862.

Gilson, Etienne. *History of Christian Philosophy in the Middle Ages.* New York: Random House, 1955. Actually starts with the first patristic apologists so is a history of Christian apologetics from the second century to the Reformation.

Macquarrie, John. *Twentieth Century Religious Thought.* New York: Harper & Row, 1963.

Pünger, B. *History of the Christian Philosophy of Religion from the Reformation to Kant.* Edinburgh: T. & T. Clark, 1887.

Reid, J. K. S. *Christian Apologetics.* Grand Rapids: William B. Eerdmans, 1969.

Tillich, Paul. *History of Christian Thought.* Edited by Carl E. Braaten. New York: Harper & Row, 1968. Rich in philosophical elements.

II
An Outline of a System of Christian Apologetics

Section 3: The Logical Starting Point in Christian Apologetics

In recent philosophical writing the word *logic* is used three different ways.

(1) Logic may refer very strictly to the manipulation of formal logical symbols and operations. For example, in symbolic logic no reference is ever made to an object or a thing or a quality. Language is restricted to symbols (for example, A, B, C, or x, y, z, etc.) and operations with symbols (as conjunction or disjunction, etc.).

(2) Logic may mean the practical or empirical use of a certain amount of formal logic, hence, applied logic. Science is the most common example of applied logic.

(3) Logic may mean the careful and systematic analysis of what we mean by words, or sentences, or what kind of presuppositions are implied in a theory, or how a philosophy or a political theory or a religion is put together and how it is argued. In this sense logic is close to reasoning where reasoning means a responsible and self-critical approach to any problem or theory in contrast to hunches, guesses, general opinion, or feelings.

Although reference will be made to logic in all three senses, the bulk of this exposition will refer to logic as it is more or less equivalent to reasoning. In philosophical terminology logic, or reasoning, refers to what Plato called the *dialectic*.

The logical status for religious belief. The factors, circumstances, and experiences that lead to a person's acceptance of a philosophy or a political theory or a religion are one thing; the truth of what the person believes is another thing. A man may have a religious experience with many attending psychological fireworks, yet the religion he accepts may be false; or a man may very quietly accept the truth. Religion is held in integrity only if it is believed to be true and if some attempt is made to show on what grounds it is held to be true.

Different kinds of theories or propositions are determined as true or false by different means. The problem for the man of faith is to determine what kind of proof proves a religion to be true. In the spectrum of truth, or among the species of methods of proof, is the manner in which a religion is to be assessed as true or false. The logical status of religious belief means the examination of methods of proof or verification or falsification that pertain particularly to the nature of religion. Proving that the tensile strength of a piece of wire is one hundred pounds involves a very different procedure than claiming that some philosophy such as materialism is true.

An acceptance of a theorem in mathematics or geometry or logic is compelled in the sense that if the demonstration is correct the conclusion follows of necessity. There is no alternative. There is an element of compulsion in the sciences, but it is not as strong a compulsion as that in mathematics or logic. If the theories are adequately stated and verified by proper experiments, every scientist who knows his science is compelled to accept the theory. But in this case alternate theories are conceivable. For example, one scientist may think that cancer is caused by a virus; another, by a chemical introduced in the processing of food products. Scientific theories do compel but without the complete exclusion of alternate answers as in formal logic.

History and sociology are put together more loosely than chemistry or physics. The factors are so complex, their interpretation subjected to many options, and verification is more uncertain. Neither historian nor sociologist works within the limits of precision required in physics. No measurement in history or sociology compares to the angstrom unit in physics. An angstrom unit is one hundred-millionth of a centimeter and is used to measure light waves.

Consequently, in history and sociology more alternative interpretations are possible, and, therefore, there may be more differences in basic theory. Furthermore, such theories cannot be verified within the close tolerances of chemistry and physics. Theories in history or sociology are, therefore, more difficult to verify. They do not carry such high probability status as theories in pure science. They cannot command assent with the same vigor as can be commanded in the basic sciences. They must allow for larger tolerances, and they admit the element of personal choice in decision making to a far higher degree than in the pure sciences.

In philosophy and religion the subject matters are so removed from simple observation, simple experimentation, simple facts, and easy control of the data that the factor of compulsion almost disappears. If there are processes of verification in philosophy and religion, they are far more complex, far more general, and contain far more variation than any of the sciences. One is compelled to say that with reference to philosophies and religions verification from the logical perspective is a choice.

In the sense that logic is defined in the preceding paragraphs, to be a Christian is to choose Christianity, or, one is a Christian by choice. It cannot be too strongly emphasized that this word *choice* must be understood in the context of logical analysis and not in the psychological sense of an arbitrary or purely personal decision.

From the standpoint of logical analysis, the Christian has the right to choose Christianity as his religion. Such a choice does not make it true, but it does remind those who are skeptical of Christianity or who reject it that they cannot deny the right of choice to the Christian. Therefore the Christian claims his right to choice as granted to all philosophers and theologians.

However, choices in philosophy or religion may be irresponsible. Although all choices are permitted, only responsible choices are worthy of consideration. A responsible choice complies with at least two criteria.

(1) The choice must be made on the basis of at least a representative survey of the great options. One may make a right choice without it being a responsible one from the perspective of the logical status of religious belief. The Christian faith is affirmed as the true religion of God, but the layman has not read the history of philosophy nor has he studied comparative religions; so although his decision is the right one, he cannot show on logical grounds (as the special use of logic has been explained in this area) that his decision is true. But the Christian apologist must show that he has had significant interaction with competing options. When his choice is made within the context of these options, it is a responsible choice.

(2) The choice must concern itself with entailment. *Entailment* is a word used by philosophers to indicate the implications of any theory or

belief. In a sense all of Christian apologetics is but a delineation of the meaning of entailment for the Christian. Entailment means exploring what one is committed to in accepting any particular belief. And no choice of any kind is a responsible one if the entailment of the choice has not been investigated. To be a Christian, for example, means to accept the authority of Holy Scripture and to accept doctrines that are very complex and difficult to explain such as the Trinity, the Incarnation, and original sin.

The Christian apologist claims that he makes a responsible choice, for he has studied Christian theology as much as he has studied philosophy and apologetics and knows in considerable detail what the entailment is in choosing the Christian faith.

The right of postulation in Christian apologetics. Individual facts, no matter how many of them, do not constitute effective knowledge. Facts must be interpreted, and the interpretation is stated in the form of a theory, a hypothesis, a generalization, or a law. This is true whether one is considering physics or philosophy.

In the days when Freud was a medical student, people with neuroses or psychoses were sent to doctors because their neuroses or psychoses were manifested in physical symptoms. The doctors in turn wrote lengthy descriptions of these symptoms. Piling up medical reports which contained mountains of facts led to no cures. The general assumption was that something was wrong somewhere in the nervous system of the patient and that something had not as yet been detected.

Certain experiences of Freud with some patients led him to think differently than the rest of the doctors. He began to take the facts and work on a theory. One could say that when Freud stopped merely recording physical symptoms of neurotic people and began to imagine theories, modern psychiatry was born. Out of his theorizing emerged such concepts as the unconscious, infant sexuality, repression, and psychosexual developments. Then cures began to take place. Facts were now seen in the context of a theory and unified by theory. The question is not whether Freud was right or wrong. The point is he tried to bring facts into a theoretical interpretation.

All progress in knowledge of any kind is possible only if from facts we go on to postulation, namely, suggesting some theory or hypothesis that integrates and explains the facts.

The Christian postulates that the Christian faith is true. This does not make Christianity true. But the Christian cannot test the truth of his faith, nor can he construct an apologetics, until he sets forth his postulate. Christianity may be false, but no philosopher or any other scholar can prevent the Christian from making his postulate. There can be no a priori rejection of the right of the Christian to make his postulate.

The logical status of any philosophy or religion is that it involves choices and postulates. The Christian faith is the choice and the postulate of the Christian.

Section 4: The Christian Postulate

The postulate *Christianity is true* is too general because there are different versions of Christianity. A Christianity that is mystically understood would develop a very different apologetics than a Christianity understood as a rational theism.

The postulate *the Holy Scriptures are true* is subject to the same ambiguity. Different kinds of theology have been derived from Holy Scripture, and different theologies mean different apologetics. An Arminian-oriented apologetics will vary significantly from a Calvinistic apologetics. Even to say that Christian theology is true is to end up having to choose among alternate theologies. Thomas Aquinas's optimism about the powers of human reason differs radically from Luther's pessimism about reason outside the illumination of the Holy Spirit.

For the discussion of Christian apologetics in this book, a particular definition of the Christian faith is presumed. Only when this is done can Christian apologetics be adequately discussed. The definition of Christianity we shall use may be expressed in a general definition and in a specific definition.

General definition: The Christian religion is the redemptive and revelatory work of the Holy Trinity which reaches its highest expression in revelation and redemption in the Incarnation of God in Christ; and this religion is preserved for all ages and is witnessed for all ages in the inspired Holy Scripture.

Specific definition: The truest expression of the Christian religion is the Reformed faith which seeks to preserve the best of Christian theology from the end of the Apostolic Age to the Reformation, and which cast the faith of the Reformation in its most biblical form.

This means the attempt to preserve the best in the Apostles Creed, the Nicene-Constantinople Creed, the Chalcedonian Creed, and the Athanasian Creed. It means paying special attention to those men who are counted as giants among the theologians and to the books that are considered classic expositions of great doctrines.

The word *Reformed* refers to the tradition of theology founded by Zwingli in the Swiss Reformation (1523) which in turn was expounded by the theological genius of John Calvin and has been further expounded and expanded in succeeding centuries and in other countries.

In making such definitions and taking such a specific position, no narrowness is intended because much overlap is involved. Many great doctrines are held in common by all the parties of the Reformation. Although they might disagree at a particular point, they agree in the general expression of the doctrine. Hence, the stance in this book has a genuine ecumenical flavor to it. Nevertheless, an effective apologetics must work with a specific understanding of the Christian religion.

Taking a historic and Reformed position in theology means that this apologetics will have a character that reflects this kind of theology. If one takes this position in theology, then his apologetics will have the following characteristics.

Christian apologetics must be grounded in divine revelation, particularly special or soteric (saving) *revelation.* From the standpoint of theory of knowledge, that is, how we know what we know, Christianity is a religion of revelation. And, in that man is a sinner in spiritual darkness, he needs a revelation aimed at dispelling that darkness. Hence, he needs special or soteric revelation.

As far as the Christian apologist is concerned, Holy Scripture is the book of revelation. God certainly has made many revelations not recorded in Holy Scripture, but operationally or functionally the apologist is limited to Holy Scripture.

To the Christian apologist, the Holy Scripture is the Word of God. This expresses the origin of Scripture, namely, God's revealing activities. It may also be called the revealed Word of God indicating that the burden of its content is revelation. It may be called the inspired Word of God to indicate how it materially or factually came into existence through men moved by the Holy Spirit. It may be called the authoritative Word of God to indicate that it comes from an authoritative person. namely, God, the highest and greatest and most perfect Being. This God is a God of truth, and therefore his revelation possesses the authority that truth possesses.

This strong emphasis on revelation does not mean the exclusion of other knowledge. For example, it is impossible to work in apologetics at any depth without an articulate knowledge of philosophy. Because so much of Scripture is historical in character, the apologist must have some working knowledge of the science of historiography and the various theories of the character of historical knowledge.

In starting with divine revelation, the Christian affirms that he is defending a religion which has come into existence through God's grace, through God's wisdom, through God's power, and not through the learning, cleverness, or unusual experiences of men.

Such an apologetics is a scriptural apologetics. This means that an effort is made to find out if the Scriptures contain a theory of self-verification. This method is in contrast with the method usually followed in a philosophy of religion or a philosophical theology. Some philosophy or philosophical system is taken as the best philosophy of the times, and from it the apologist works his way to Christianity and the Scriptures. Today some apologists take existentialism or process philosophy or analytic philosophy as their normative framework of reference and then work their way to Scripture.

To the contrary our method is to look into the Scripture first and determine if it sets forth any fundamental apologetic theses that any apologetic that calls itself Christian must incorporate within itself. God's revelation is larger than Holy Scripture, but the only revelation at our command is Holy Scripture, and, therefore, to Scripture we must go first to determine what a Christian apologetics must contain.

Some apologists have defended a Christological apologetics. Jesus Christ is to them the supreme vindication of Christianity. But the only Christ we know is the Christ of the New Testament. A Christological apologetics not grounded in the New Testament revelation is an impossibility. A Christ separated from Scripture is a nameless, faceless, religious cipher.

Others have maintained an apologetics of the Holy Spirit. If the Spirit speaks in our hearts, we are told, then we will know that our faith is truth. But who knows a line about the Holy Spirit apart from Holy Scripture? An apologetics of the Holy Spirit that does not draw its materials from Holy Scripture is not a Christian apologetics, for Christians are allowed to recognize only the Spirit revealed in Scripture. A Holy Spirit separated from Scripture is a religious notion or a philosophical assumption but in any case is devoid of power to show that the biblical revelation is true.

Such an apologetics is a Trinitarian apologetics. Christian apologetics is based upon Christian theology. Christian theology centers in a particular doctrine of revelation and in a particular doctrine of salvation. Revelation is Trinitarian in its structure. God the Father speaks; the Son is the content of what the Father speaks; and the Spirit is the One who illuminates the human heart so that it can see revelation as God's truth. Redemption or salvation is Trinitarian. God the Father plans and decrees salvation; the Son is the One who dies in time and space on this earth as the divine sacrifice for the sins of men; the Spirit is the One who applies this salvation in the heart of the believer.

Although it will not be repeated in the successive pages, it is to be understood that the God in this apologetics is the Trinitarian God with the full implication that involves. An apologetics that seeks to be solely a Christological apologetics or solely an apologetics of the Holy Spirit is a curtailed apologetics. The God who acts and speaks in Scripture is the Father and the Son and the Holy Spirit. If God's speech and God's acts are the substance of Christian theology, then our apologetics must be Trinitarian. Otherwise our apologetics becomes nothing more than a philosophy of religion with a thin veneer of Christianity painted on it.

Such an apologetics is in the Augustinian, Anselmic, Lutheran, and Calvinistic tradition. This tradition has certain features which all of these men held in common.

(1) Divine revelation has priority over human philosophy. No philosophy is more fundamental than Holy Scripture nor has a position prior to divine revelation. No philosophy is the necessary correlate of Christian revelation even though apologists must use philosophy. Christian revelation is the higher critic of all philosophies whenever they impinge on the knowledge of God.

(2) Human depravity affects the will of man and the passions of man making him weak in temptation and pushing him into sin. Sin affects the mind of man, especially with reference to God and the knowledge of God. Man is a theologically darkened sinner. Human reason does not escape the damaging effects of sin. It is indeed strange and enigmatic that a number of contemporary theologians (new liberals, advocates of the death of God movement, process theologians) deny that sin materially affects the mind of the sinner and therefore of the theologian or philosopher or apologist. This neo-Pelagianism seems incredible after Freud and Hitler. It is even more incredible if one studies the history of war and the history of penal institutions.

In his work *The Condition of the Christian Philosopher*,[1] Roger Mehl

---

1. Philadelphia: Fortress Press, 1963.

shows how seriously the Reformers reckoned with the effects of sin on the rational processes of man. This problem cannot be so easily dismissed as many recent theologians have done. With our knowledge of psychiatry today, how can a person claim that we think free from all pressures? All of us have our defense mechanisms, our cultural conditioning, and our deceptive acts of rationalization. What is this theologically but the effects of sin? How then can a modern theologian believe that he can think in a completely neutral, mental atmosphere?

(3) If man is a sinner, he needs the purification of the mind to see the truth. The gospel is received in faith. The gospel received in faith brings the purification of the heart and the illumination of the mind. In this sense, then, we believe in order to understand.

Augustine had a very special theory of learning. He believed that the basis of learning was love. If the student thoroughly hates the teacher, how much does the student learn? If the student loves the teacher, how readily does he learn? According to Augustine, there is no learning without love, and therefore the basis of any theory of learning is love. How can a man know God, asks Augustine. If man loves God, he will know God. But only in redemption does man come to love God; and once redeemed and now loving God, man comes to know God. Therefore, as faith brings redemption, it brings love, and with love comes understanding.

But understanding must come. One cannot be a Fideist and rest on his sheer experience of faith, never moving beyond that point. The Fideist refuses to look for evidence beyond his experience of faith. One cannot be a mystic in the sense that he relies solely on his mystical experience and never attempts to correlate it with Holy Scripture, Christian theology, and what may be learned from psychology. One cannot hold on dearly to the seven fundamentals of the faith and never press on to the fullness of the counsel of God in all of Scripture nor cease to interact responsibly with other areas of human knowledge.

The kind of Christian apologetics set forth here calls for the best in Christian scholarship particularly from those Christians who have the educational background and mental abilities to do this. Faith brings us to salvation, but faith coming to understanding is a process that is continuous throughout the life of the Christian.

"Faith leads, the intellect follows" is a special kind of rationalism. It is not the rationalism of a philosophical theology or of a natural theology. It is not the rationalism of the Deists or the men of the Enlightenment who placed human reason as judge over divine revelation and never measured the impact of sin on their reasoning powers. It is a rationalism that recognizes the authority of revelation and the depraving effects of sin. It is a rationalism that knows of man's need for the illumination of the Spirit and reckons with the transcendence, mystery, and incomprehensibility of God. However, within these conditions and qualifications it does seek the profoundest understanding of Christian theology possible by means of every conceivable source of knowledge that bears on the biblical revelation and its specific texts.

Section 5: Circle One—The Persuasion and Witness of the Holy Spirit

The verification of the Christian faith can be outlined in the pattern of three concentric circles. These circles do not have sharp lines. They may blend into each other at points and even double back on each other. But they do represent three stages in the process of verification which shows on what grounds Christianity is held to be true.

There is no clear doctrine of the witness of the Holy Spirit in the history of theology until the time of the Reformation. Augustine's theory of illumination with reference to salvation and revelation is an anticipation of the doctrine.[2] Thomas Aquinas's light of faith (which has become part of Roman Catholic theology) is another anticipation.

When Luther responded to Erasmus in *The Bondage of the Will*, he discussed the clarity of Scripture. This was a matter of great debate at the time of the Reformation. How do we make the Scriptures clear? How do we shed light on difficult or obscure passages? Does the Roman Catholic church have special grace in this regard? Luther answered that the clarity of Scripture was in two phases. (1) The *grammatical clarity* of Scripture meant that Scripture could be interpreted according to the customary laws of language. Philological exegesis was competent to make sense out of Scripture if any sense could be made. (2) The *spiritual clarity* of Scripture was the illumination of the mind of the believer by the Holy Spirit. Augustine had struggled at this point too and made Christ the internal Teacher of all Christians. Luther was closer to the biblical text at this point in naming the Holy Spirit as the internal Teacher of all Christians. But Luther did not develop this doctrine of the

---

2. R. H. Nash, *The Light of the Mind: St. Augustine's Theory of Knowledge* (Lexington: University Press of Kentucky, 1969).

Holy Spirit in any significant way apart from his special use of it in *The Bondage of the Will.*

John Calvin forged the relevant scriptural passages about the work of the Spirit into a theology of the witness of the Spirit. The fundamental treatment is in the first nine chapters of the first book of *The Institutes of the Christian Religion.*

Calvin's basic thesis was: divine things can be known as divine things only by a divine means. Conversely, divine things cannot be attested by human means. Or, in yet other terms, a divine revelation by the very fact that it is divine cannot be verified by something exterior to it but only by its internal nature.

Calvin found support in such Scriptures as Romans 8:14–16; Galatians 4:6; 1 Corinthians 1–2; 2 Corinthians 3:3, 4:6; and 1 John 4:13, 5:1–10, 20. He therefore felt that his doctrine of Christian certainty was derived from the revelation in Holy Scripture itself and that he was not imposing a principle outside of Scripture upon Christian theology. The witness of the Spirit is the divine persuasion about divine things.

Calvin would say that if the church tells a person that Christianity is true, this is a human witness because it would only be men, even if religious men, telling a person that Christianity is true.

If a theologian attempted to verify Christianity by unaided reason or a particular philosophy, this too would be only a human validation.

If a person claimed to have a radical or unusual experience of God (for example, the Anabaptists), Calvin would say that this too is only human verification.

If a person argued from Christian evidences, this would be of little help since evidences are seen as evidences only after man's mind is illuminated by faith. Until then all evidences are equivocal or ambiguous.

Only the witness of the Holy Spirit is able to bear the kind of burden imposed on the Christian at the point of the validation of the Christian faith.

In Greek history a witness first meant a person who could tell another person or a court of law of facts that he knew by personal observation. Thus the facts of the witness became the facts of the court and were treated as if the court itself were the observer.

Then the word *witness* picked up a second aspect. To witness meant to persuade the court that the facts were true facts. The report of the observations was accompanied by the persuasion that the facts reported were true facts.

The Holy Spirit is a witness in both meanings of the word *witness,* and one of the discoveries of the study of the Holy Spirit in this century is to show the juridical or forensic character of much of the work of the Holy Spirit. This aspect of the work of the Spirit had gone undetected or unappreciated in the older books on the Holy Spirit.

Persuasion is the effort to convince somebody that something is true. Genuine persuasion never resorts to unethical methods. The Holy Spirit is the Divine Persuader, and he persuades only in the context of truth. He is the witness to the believer that the gospel is true and persuades the believer that the gospel is true.

The product of the witnessing and persuading of the Holy Spirit in the believer is a state of certainty, a sense of coming into the truth of God. Paul describes this state by the use of the Greek word *plērophoria*, "fullness of conviction, having the sense or feeling of being persuaded of the truth." Hence, the Christian comes to the conclusion that the gospel he believes is the truth of God, and he knows this through the conviction and persuasion of the Holy Spirit.

This is the kind of certainty of the faith that all believers have even though they are not conscious of the witnessing of the Holy Spirit. In fact, most of them do not even know of the doctrine of the witness of the Spirit. This does not mean, however, that they have not received the witness of the Spirit. The Spirit does not direct his activity toward himself but toward the gospel, toward Christ, and toward Holy Scripture. The believer is aware of a sense of certainty, of a sense of divine sonship, and of having found the truth, and these are the products of the witness of the Holy Spirit. Thus all Christians have the witness of the Spirit. The witness of the Spirit does not require a knowledge of theology or apologetics or philosophy. It is an integral part of the experience of the gospel.

In Roman Catholic apologetics only philosophers can follow the arguments for the faith. Hence, a real knowledge that Christianity is true is reserved for those people with enough education to follow the arguments. The rest of the Roman Catholic church must be satisfied with "passive infallibility"—although himself fallible, the Catholic Christian believes in an infallible church. The doctrine of the witness of the Spirit does not restrict certainty of faith to professors.

Whereas the Roman Catholic apologists found the fundamental verification of their faith in a philosophical system external to the faith yet being congruent with it, the Reformers chose to rest their faith within Scripture, or more precisely, in the verification of Christianity taught by the Scriptures themselves. In older language the Christian faith was *autopistic*. In this connection *auto* means "itself" and *pistic* (from the

Greek word for faith) means "believable." Christianity is credible, believable, within itself and therefore need not depend on externals for verification.

The kind of apologetics defended in this book avoids the problematic distinction between historic faith and saving faith. In Roman Catholicism historic faith is called the Preamble to Faith which means the creation of a favorable disposition toward revealed truth. In Protestantism historic faith is again a favorable disposition created for the gospel by Christian evidences or theistic proofs. Once a person has historic faith he is then in a position to hear the gospel and move on to saving faith. Such an approach presents a whole nest of problems.

The Reformers made the witness of the Spirit part of the structure of saving faith so that the experience of salvation and the sense of the certainty of faith are bound up in the same event. I believe this structure is found in the New Testament itself.

At this point it might appear that the witness of the Spirit is a disguised form of subjectivism. But this is not the case. In the older representations theologians said that the witness of the Spirit was "in the Word." That is, no alleged Christian experience was considered genuine if it was not anchored in Holy Scripture. Some cults jump when they feel the Spirit and others roll. The witness of the Spirit is not in the jump or the roll but in the Word. This gives the doctrine of the witness of the Spirit an external reference point and also a critical foundation for the assessment of any so-called experience of the gospel.

The witness in the Word means that the first message of Holy Scripture is Jesus Christ and his gospel. Men become Christians through faith in Christ. The Holy Spirit bears his original witness at this point. Thus the gospel, Jesus Christ and his salvation, and the witness of the Spirit are all one piece. This is the meaning of 1 John 5:8—"There are three witnesses, the Spirit, the water, and the blood; and these three agree" (RSV). The expression *water and blood* is taken metaphorically to describe the life of Christ as bounded at one end by his baptism (water) and at the other end by his death (blood). Thus the gospel facts represent the external fulcrum of the witness of the Spirit in which the Spirit gives a persuasion in the spirit of the believer witnessing to the reality of his salvation.

This external-internal structure of the Spirit's witness prevents subjectivism, religious individualism, or a Christianity based on pure experience.

In the past the entire Christian apologetics has been rested on the uniqueness of Jesus Christ. For example, his moral teaching is the highest in human history, his own moral perfection or holiness or sinlessness is unmatched in any other religion, the quality of his words impressed listeners as being the Word of God, his teaching about God is the purest theism ever propounded by man, and he sealed the divine character of his origin, life, and teachings by his resurrection from the dead. This is acceptable as far as it goes and is the basis on which the believer says by the help of the Spirit that "Jesus is Lord" (1 Cor. 12:3, RSV). Second Corinthians 3:12–18 also expresses that the Christian beholds the glory of God in Jesus Christ. But an apologetics which has such a strong emotional appeal to Christians needs further shoring up if it is really to stand as an apologetic. The revelation in Holy Scripture and the action of the Holy Spirit cannot be eliminated from any apologetic, even a Christological one.

The work of the Holy Spirit as witness and as persuader is an analogy taken from juridical procedures. But there is another model of the witness of the Spirit which comes from what might be called the realm of the intellectual or of knowledge or of learning. In this model the witness of the Spirit is illumination.

Illumination is seeing the truth of God as the truth of God. It does not necessarily mean new information. A person may know all the facts beforehand. It is not their newness that constitutes illumination. Nor is illumination the rational comprehension of what heretofore was puzzling. It is seeing something as true, whether it was well known or unknown. The Holy Spirit enables the believer to see the revelation of God as the truth of God. To go through such an experience in which the gospel becomes the truth of God "for you" is to undergo illumination of the Spirit. This is the corollary of the witness of the Spirit within the imagery of light. The goal of illumination is *plērophoria*—the state of being convinced that something is true.

Those who are pure in heart see God (Matt. 5:8). This means that the vision of God is possible only on spiritual grounds, not rational or philosophical grounds. Illumination is then something that happens with saving faith in which there is forgiveness of sins which is in turn the purification of the heart. Then the sinner sees God. *Seeing* is a visual term, an intuitional term. It means a direct grasp or apprehension of something in contrast to knowing something through logical processes such as induction or deduction. The Hebrew concept of knowing connotes an intimacy that is lacking in the English language. *To know a woman* is a euphemism for sexual experience. Knowing means participation as well as understanding. Illumination contains this additional Semitic element lacking in the English word. Further, although the realization of truth comes through the witness of the Spirit or the illumination of the Spirit, it is not a nonrational or an irrational experience. The mind is at work and must be at work. But it is at work within the matrix of ideas and events which includes the Holy Spirit as well as not excluding the rational processes of the mind.

The illumination of the Spirit in the spirit of the believer is the reverse of Paul's description of the effects of sin in man as described in Romans 1:19–32. In this passage Paul shows that the further man plunges himself into sin the more obscure and clouded becomes his knowledge of God. The sinner who once worshiped God in his true spirituality ends up worshiping an idol. The illumination of the Spirit reverses this. As man comes to God in faith and in salvation, he regains the right concept of God, for in this experience he sees God for what he truly is.

The witness of the Spirit is not a separate experience but part of the experience of the gospel. Paul states that the gospel is the power of God (Rom. 1:16; 1 Cor. 2:4, 4:20; 1 Thess. 1:5). That is, when the gospel is believed, it really does something to the believer. Believing the gospel is a transition from one belief to another and involves rational elements. But it is more than a transition of one's allegiance. Believing the gospel creates new attitudes such as conviction, repentance, and trust. It gives one a sense of the forgiveness of sin and a power to redirect one's life toward righteousness. It moves the sinner from spiritual apathy and lethargy or indifference to a positive life of prayer and devotion with God. He is born again; he receives a divine nature; he receives afresh the image of God; he is the new man. All of these concepts are concepts of power and so forbid any interpretation that makes faith a dry, powerless act of the intellect.

Part of the work of the Spirit in salvation then is to release in the heart of the believer the power of the gospel, and this experience of power becomes another assurance that what one believes is the truth of God.

The New Testament not only makes it clear that faith is a transforming act but that the gospel accepted in faith is the true gospel. This Paul expresses in 1 Corinthians 15:1–7. There is a Greek expression in verse 3 that loses the full force of its meaning in translation. It is the expression *en prótois*. The word *prótos* has three meanings: in reference to space, it means to be in front; in reference to time, it means to be first; in reference to importance, it means to be the most important. Paul uses it in this third sense. What he lists are the most important elements of the gospel, that is, he tells us what the true gospel is. The right saving gospel includes saving faith.

The New Testament not only calls for right doctrine for salvation, but it demands a moral and spiritual change in the one who confesses his faith in Christ and the doctrines of the gospel. God sheds his love abroad in the hearts of believers (Rom. 5:5). If the mark of a believer is the love of God filling the heart of a person, one must question the validity of the beliefs of a person who does not exhibit love for God and love for man. No man is to be taken at his word. In 1 John the phrase *if a man says* is repeated (1:6, 2:4, 2:9) to indicate that if there is a contradiction between what a man says and what he does he doesn't bear the marks of a true Christian. Further, Paul gives a list of notorious sins and indicates that the kind of person who persists in doing these things does not inherit the kingdom of God (Gal. 5:21).

Only those claims to faith which are based on right doctrine and right living are genuine. This is not to say that the church knows infallibly who believes the right way or who is living the right way. Only God truly knows the heart of man. But a Christian can detect in the daily life of another confessing Christian some elements that indicate the character of the person's spirituality and at least make a preliminary distinction between sheep and goats.

To sum up, Circle One includes the following: (1) Every Christian has the witness of the Spirit which persuades him that his faith is in the truth; (2) this persuasion has external anchorage in the Word of God and the redemptive acts of Christ; (3) it functions verificationally in that it is a witness of a revealed Word and a redemptive history and the persuasion that both are true; (4) it is a spiritual verification in that the primary verification of religion must be of this order else the case is deeded away to a method of verification alien to religion. In other terms, only God can speak for God. This we consider fundamental and not negotiable for Christian apologetics. The witness of the Spirit alone meets this requirement.

III

An Outline of a System of Christian Apologetics (continued)

Section 6: Circle Two—The Action of God in Creation and History

The witness of the Spirit in the spirit of the believer is adequate as far as it goes, and most Christians find their intellectual or rational peace in this witness. This is not subjectivism. Subjectivism in its most objectionable sense is the thesis that what a person believes is true simply because he believes it or that a person affirms something as true because of his own unique experience. This makes as many truths as there are people, for if we canonize truth by our experiences, the next person has equal rights to canonize his experiences. If we introduce criteria to separate real experiences from bad experiences, we have forsaken verification by experience and moved into those criteria which divide the true from the false experiences.

In recent theological literature *subjectivity* (coming from Kierkegaard) is that kind of truth that is inward without being subjectivism. The witness of the Spirit is, according to this terminology, subjectivity but not subjectivism. A man who loves a woman for her beauty, charm, wit, personality, etc., has love as subjectivity; the man who loves a woman because he is in love with love is guilty of subjectivism.

Christianity is more than gospel, it is more than faith as subjectivity, and it is more than the witness of the Spirit. There are objective elements in Holy Scripture, and there are other criteria of truth in philosophy. Therefore, apologetics must advance beyond the witness of the Spirit if it seeks to be a comprehensive Christian apologetics.

The internal witness of the Spirit in the heart of the believer and objectively, in the sense of the point of reference, is in the Word. But *Word* in this sense means gospel. By extension it becomes the total Word of God. This transition from the narrow meaning of Word as gospel to Word as Holy Scripture I have traced in my book *The Witness of the Spirit.*

But there are other criteria in Holy Scripture which witness to its divine origin and therefore to its truthfulness.

The living God acts in our world and in our history. In the Old Testament, God is very rarely called the true God. This mode of thinking was not quite proper to that culture. Rather God is presented as the living God. The living God acts in time, in events, in the lives of people, and so makes a difference. In logic a proposition that doesn't make a difference is not a proposition, and in science a theory with no operational consequences is not a theory. So in theology a definition or concept of God in which the existence of such a God makes no difference is not God. Only the living God makes a difference and is a God in whom we can believe and in our later categories of expression call the true God.

"Why is there something and not nothing?" To some this is the greatest question of modern man. Or in Camus's more dramatic words, "Why should I not commit suicide?" The Christian answer at the first level is the doctrine of creation. There is something and not nothing because God created, and in this creation he makes a difference. The answer to Camus is that this creation is a good creation and is worth living for rather than dying to escape.

In more theological terms, the universe is God's witness, God's general revelation, and God's self-testimony that as Creator he is Lord, living and true. To keep the exposition clear, the Creator of Genesis 1 is also the God and Father of Jesus Christ our Lord. Thus creation is the original act of God as the living God, the acting God, the revealing God. *The God who makes a difference.* Therefore he is a God about whom we can make assertions that are real and not metaphysical abstractions. If this God did not create, there would be no universe nor would you and I exist.

God also participates in our history. Holy Scripture is not limited to theological discussions or theological revelations but reveals that the God who creates is also a God of providence and a God of history. Therefore he acts in history and makes a difference. There would never have been a nation called Israel if God had not acted in history and called Abraham. Out of the actions of a living God issue historical events that would otherwise never have occurred.

Because God acted in creation and because he acts in history, the Christian knows he worships a living God and that he has the Word of the living God. This is the background and this is the presupposition of all Scripture, of all Christian theology, and of all Christian apologetics.

The verification of Christianity through the witness of the Spirit needs the supplementation of the action of the living God in creation and history. Otherwise the witness of the Spirit, standing alone, looks too much like a piece of subjectivism. When the divine action in creation and history is added to the witness of the Spirit, the latter loses its threat of being called only a subjective experience.

For apologetical purposes the creation of the universe by God and the providential guidance of history by God are too general. There is not enough bite in them to show that these are truly God's actions. The Christian in his theology and reading of Scripture sees these matters as realities and this is not to be contested. However, in apologetics the strongest kind of divine action must be appealed to. There must be some outcropping of the supernatural. This is the real bite in God's actions.

When God acts supernaturally, he truly comes into our cosmos, our world, our experience. Furthermore, when he comes in some supernatural way, we really know that he has come. Christian theologies that prune off the supernatural degenerate into mere religious philosophies. As sophisticated and learned and modern and enlightened and scientific as these philosophies wish to represent themselves, they do so at the enormous price of presenting a Christianity that does not make a difference. Although such theologies may have an intellectual appeal of great strength (for example, Tillich) there is no real bite, no real unequivocal action of God, and therefore they possess no means of showing that what they claim is the Word of God is in reality the Word of God.

Nor can it be argued that supernaturalism is out of date or unbelievable in the twentieth century. Supernatural events are events. If they are of this order, they happened or they didn't. If they happened, then they are a solid part of history. A miracle cannot be undone because modern man has no room for miracles in his mentality. Nor can a miracle be undone by saying that in the eighteenth century miracles were a help to faith but the intellectual climate has so changed that miracles are now a hindrance to the modern man, ergo, they never really happened.

Miracles are not in the same class as ethical principles. The Romans had no apprehension about exposing to death unwanted or unliked babies. To leave one's baby to die in a patch of bushes would be a serious crime today. The intellectual or cultural atmosphere does make many older attitudes and morals obsolete. But events are not subject to intellectual climates for verification. Granted, theories of historiography (the set of principles whereby a historian works with his materials and interprets them) do change, and the kinds of possible events are judged differently by different historiographies.

Another element mentioned in older works on Christian evidences but dropped out of modern discussions is the pragmatic or functional service of the supernatural. It is currently argued that miracles are a hindrance to faith and not a help. This means that they create more philosophical problems than they help establish religious truths.

What prophet of the Old Testament had the learning or time to discuss at great length the theological issues in faith in the Lord? What time and circumstances were available to Christ that he might lecture on the truth of the revelation he was bringing? Or, how could Paul teach a pagan audience in Galatia with learned theological discourse? Modern man may have his problems with the supernatural, and it might take a year of lectures to get any sympathetic response from him. But in Old Testament days, the days of Christ, and the days of the apostles, there was not the time, nor the learning in lecturer nor listener to advance an articulate apologetic of faith. Something had to function in these situations that would immediately and directly accomplish the necessary goal, namely, clearly demonstrate that the man who is speaking is speaking God's Word. This the supernatural does.

If a scholar objects to the supernatural on whatever ground, at least pragmatically and situationally there is nothing he can suggest that can function with the same power and immediacy as the supernatural. If a modern scholar does not see this problem, then he is thinking so academically, unrealistically, and unhistorically, that what he says does not really speak significantly to the issue.

As a historian he may believe on principle that miracles do not happen. This is not difficult to understand when one reads some Greek, Roman, and early church literature. The ancient world did view the supernatural in ways we would regard today as fictional. In fact it is a real surprise to students to find in Luther's *Tabletalk* a lot of nonsense about the supernatural that Luther believed. At this point Calvin was far more cautious than Luther. But if an event is an event, then historiographical principles as such, in themselves, cannot unmake the event. Historians may be skeptical of the event, but attitudes about history cannot change the realities of history.

Whether one believes in the supernatural or not is very much governed by the mood of the century of the historian. The climate of opinion in some historical periods dictates that some things are not credible. For the Christian, the miracles recorded in Holy Scripture are not to be judged by cultural moods or climates of opinion but are to be assessed in terms of the kind of role or function they had in their day and the kind of attestation they have.

From the very earliest days of Christian apologetics, miracles, fulfilled prophecies, and the resurrection of Christ were sure indicia that the Christian religion was the true religion of God. Eventually these topics were described as Christian evidences, a topic we shall return to later. But at the present time this argument has taken a significant shift in stance or position or mode of expression. The action of God in creation and history shows that the God of Holy Scripture is the living God for he makes a difference in creation and history.

The supernatural action of God in the cosmos is in the form of the miracle and supremely in the resurrection of Christ (its eschatological character sets it apart from all other miracles). In the realm of history the supernatural action of God is the fulfilled promise of God. Granted there is an enormous literature today about how the Old and New Testaments are to be related. Granted that much of the older literature about fulfilled prophecy is out of focus according to modern knowledge of the Old Testament. But the essential structure remains unchanged. That the living God makes a difference in history can be known by his realized Word or fulfilled Word (or whatever schema the Old Testament scholar chooses to use as long as he does not evaporate the fact that the Lord makes a real, detectable difference in history which would not be there if he were not a God who acted in history).

This is the kind of divine action, the kind of divine impingement upon human history that makes a difference and rebuts the charge of the analytic philosophers who contend that theological statements are empty or senseless or meaningless because they have no empirical content.

One further item: the biblical character of the supernatural is based on the fact that man is a sinner. Because ordinary ways of knowledge are rendered ambiguous by reason of man's sin, God breaks into sinful man by means of the supernatural. To discuss the supernatural outside the consideration of human sin as if the supernatural were purely an academic or theological problem is not to talk at all about the supernatural in Holy Scripture. Because God does break into his cosmos and into his history, the sinner knows that the promises made to him are not empty promises, spiritual and unverifiable, but real promises. Without such a breaking into sinful man, theological or religious or spiritual teachings would ever remain ambiguous.

The divine action of God as the living God is based on Scripture. Twentieth-century theology almost uniformly agrees that the appeal to Christian evidences went out with the coming of the Enlightenment and modern science. It is an apologetic of another century that is now outmoded. Once upon a time such reasoning appealed to people, but no more.

God's action in creation and history is not an assumption by apologists of previous centuries. It is not a theological maneuver deriving solely from man. It is the express teaching of Scripture.

Prophecy: "Set forth your *case,* says the Lord; bring your *proofs,* says the King of Jacob. Let them bring them, *and tell us what is to happen.* Tell us the former things, what they are, that we may consider them, *that we may know their outcome; or declare to us the things to come. Tell us what is to come hereafter,* that we may know that you are gods; do good, or do harm [that is, make a difference in history], that we may be dismayed and terrified" (Isa. 41:21–23, rsv, italics mine). Identical themes are expressed in Isaiah 42:9, 44:7, 48:14 and very graphically in Deuteronomy 18:15–22 where it is asserted that if a prophet cannot prophesy events which come true he is not speaking God's Word.

It is granted that some of the older works on Christian evidences had too magical a view of prophecy which has been corrected in the twentieth century. Some writers prefer the word *promise* to prophecy. And some Old Testament scholars indicate that there have been prophecies that were not fulfilled. But even with these modifications or qualifications the essential thesis that God acts in history through prophecy or promise is not basically disturbed.

Miracles: "How shall we escape if we neglect such a great salvation? It was declared at first by the Lord, and it was attested to us by those who heard him, while God also bore witness by signs and wonders and various miracles and by gifts of the Holy Spirit distributed according to his own will" (Heb. 2:3–4, rsv). This passage shows how self-conscious the writer of Hebrews was (long before any discussion of Christian evidences) of the power of miracles to attest to the veracity of the gospel message.

Resurrection of Christ: "Because he has fixed a day on which he will judge the world in righteousness by a man whom he has appointed, and of this he has given assurance to all men by raising him from the dead"

(Acts 17:31, RSV). This is no general affirmation of the resurrection of Christ but an apologetic reference. The resurrection of Christ is the assurance, the evidence in history, that God will judge the dead at some future time.

So-called Christian evidences is therefore not a strategy invented by Christians after the close of the canon. It is part of the scriptural witness to itself. This does not mean that all that has been said in the name of Christian evidences is true, nor does it mean that many suggested evidences are really evidences, such as the glorious history of the church. Church history contains much that is inglorious. But the essential argument is scriptural and not an imposition on Christian faith by apologists of some older uncritical period.

The revelations and actions of the living God are the foundations of Christian experience. Christian experience has on its inner side faith, justification, regeneration, and divine sonship. But all of these experiences are based on historical realities. It is the prior revelation and action of God which determine the character of Christian experience and warrant its authenticity. Or, to put it another way, the truth of God and the action of God are both the presupposition and the test of Christian experience. The veracity of faith is then dependent upon the action of the living God.

The Christian community has been seriously concerned with history since Augustine's *City of God*. Not every generation of Christian theologians felt this concern as they should. In the nineteenth century this concern was somewhat systematized into a theory of holy history (von Hofmann). It has been dubbed *Heilsgeschichte* (*Heil* meaning salvation; *Geschichte* meaning history). It has been defended most vigorously in modern times by Oscar Cullmann.[1] A book which brings most of modern thinking together around the general themes of history and holy history is Eric Rust's *Salvation History*.[2]

In a narrow sense *Heilsgeschichte* means a very specific theory of history and salvation; in a broad sense it means that biblical religion is not a series of revealed truths or a handbook on theology but its backbone is history. A biblical faith that abstracts history out of it is not a biblical faith. History is part of the very fiber of biblical religion. In this general sense many theologians accept the idea of *Heilsgeschichte*.

---

1. See *Christ and Time*, rev. ed. (Philadelphia: Westminster, 1964), and *Salvation in History* (New York: Harper & Row, 1967).

2. Richmond, Va.: John Knox Press, 1962.

Heilsgeschichte (used in a general way) is paralleled by *Offenbarungs-geschichte* (*Offenbarung* means revelation, hence, the history of revelation). God not only acts but he reveals; he not only does something, he says something. With the Event is the Word. The Word has as much to do with the shaping of Christian experience as the Event.

The internal witness of the Spirit is paralleled by the external actions of God in Event and Word. The Word and Event make it very clear that the witness of the Spirit is protected from becoming only an internal religious experience and nothing more; and the witness of the Spirit prevents the divine History and the divine Word from being objectified religion which can be believed for its sheer objectivity apart from the transforming power of faith and the Spirit.

The word *supernatural* has become ambiguous and needs clarification. Many older liberal theologians used the word *supernatural* simply to mean "beyond the natural order." Prayer, worship, ethics, and values were supernatural in the sense that they were not matters of physics, chemistry, or circuits of the nervous system. Thus they took a position against materialism or naturalism or positivism. The evangelical accepts this definition of the supernatural as a valid but partial one.

The concept of the supernatural in Scripture is more psychological than scientific or philosophical. The importance of the supernatural event was the psychological impact it made. From the standpoint of the ordering of nature, it may be a very natural event, but the context in which it occurs or the manner in which it occurs gives the impression that God is here now working or acting. It may be called the supernatural of the coincidence or the supernatural of the timing. Perhaps the wind or other factors we do not know of were part of the means by which Israel escaped from Egypt. But the wind and the other factors occurring at just the right time and in context of God's promised Word gave the event the character of the supernatural. At least in the minds of the Israelites it was an unusual or remarkable or supernatural act of God. Perhaps other phenomena of the preservation of the Israelites in the wilderness were of the natural order, but they occurred at such critical times and in response to their prayers or from the Word of God through Moses that to them these were direct acts of God.

(In the above paragraph I would have preferred the word *phenomenological* to *psychological*. But it is such a technical and difficult concept of philosophy that I chose the word *psychological* which all readers understand. The psychological is included in the phenomenological, but phenomenological is the more comprehensive word and the word which expresses most accurately what I have in mind.)

In this same connection, consider the event of the cross, the event of man's redemption. As a crucifixion it was an ordinary event. Some unusual phenomena were manifest at the time such as the darkness, the splitting of the veil, and the rending of the rocks. But these are never used in the remainder of the New Testament as any kind of supportive witness to the meaning of the cross. The cross is the supreme supernatural event in Scripture: the act of atonement in the death of Christ. Yet viewed externally it was not a supernatural phenomenon.

On the other hand, certain events are recorded in Scripture which would be difficult to understand apart from their being supernatural acts of God—the cleansing of a leper, the healing of cripples, the resuscitation of Lazarus, the multiplication of food, the walking on water. These were not unusual coincidences nor were they natural events with an important theological meaning. They were miraculous events in the most obvious and popular meaning of the words *miracle* and *supernatural*.

There is no question that it is hard to state the precise nature of a supernatural event without getting into some sort of logical difficulty (compare E. and M-L Keller, *Miracles in Dispute*). When the words *contrary* and *contradiction* are used in the definition of the supernatural, the case is virtually lost by virtue of the definition.

Some apologists try to resolve the problem by saying that miracles are the products of laws we do not yet know. The miracle is a rare event or an unusual event, and thus stands out. But behind it is a natural law if man could but discover it. To date he hasn't. Therefore, a miracle is not contrary to nature or science, but it is a rare event, and it is the rarity and perhaps the dramatic elements in the miracle that make it function in a special way. Theoretically there may be laws that exhibit themselves only in rare situations, but in ordinary science it is the frequence and the regularity of the data which form the basis of the generalization called a law of nature.

Augustine's explanation comes the closest to what we want to say (as his is a phenomenological definition—the miracles are described in their unusual character but their exact relationship to the world order is bracketed or suspended). He states that there is the usual, the customary, the routine, the established way in which the world runs its course. But some things happen that run a different course. We do not know their origins nor do we know the principles which govern their behavior.

Psychologically they grab us; they call attention to themselves in a magnetic way; we realize something unusual is at work. These events occur within the context of God's redemptive and revelatory work and are associated with the Word of God. So we call them wonders or signs or miracles or the great deeds of God. They clearly witness to the fact that God is here at work in our space, in our time, and in our order of nature. Hence, they disclose the reality of the Word of God, the substance of the divine promise, the concreteness of what God does for us. The Word is sealed by the act, and the act is understood by the Word.

Theology that rejects the supernatural and miraculous is only word, promise, speculation, or philosophy. It cannot assure the reality of divine action. Its adherents have made peace with the scientist and philosopher, but it has cost them the sense of the real empirical reality of divine revelation and divine salvation.

Theologians who deny the supernatural and rest their case on an existential or mystical experience or a novel way of looking at events religiously cannot show that what they believe makes a difference. They cannot show unequivocally that what they teach breaks into reality.

The same problem haunts theologians who deny the supernatural and attempt to indicate the uniqueness of Christianity by the way it uses language. This is not to deny the legitimate question of the nature of theological language. Nevertheless, men who deny the supernatural and rest their faith in the uniqueness of theological language or the special character of theological language cannot show that what their language asserts makes a difference, that it breaks into reality. They cannot meet the serious threat of Feuerbach who would say that these theologies are nothing more than man's projection of his own experiences into the cosmos. Nor can they stave off the accusation of the analytic or linguistic philosophers who assert that such diluted theological claims assert nothing because by rejecting the real action of God in the world they cannot make any empirical or significant assertions. Such antisupernatural theologies, such antimiraculous theologies simply do not make a difference in the cosmos.

The function of Christian evidences. As previously indicated, Christian evidences is not the best expression. Our fundamental concept has been the action of the living God in creation, revelation, and redemption. Items not included in the older books on Christian evidences are included in this broader definition, and many of the items in the older works on Christian evidences are no longer valid. But we have indicated that the actions of the living God come to their most unequivocal expression in the supernatural. In the following exposition we shall use the expression *Christian evidences*, but it will be meant in the broader sense we have stipulated.

The important question for Christian apologetics is what is the place of Christian evidences in Christian apologetics. The alternatives are as follows:

The *Evidentialists* (my own term) believe that Christian evidences do establish the divine origin of the Christian faith. The supernatural event validates the theological claim. A revelation is tested by reason. Reason recognizes the presence of God in the supernatural. Holy Scripture presents us with many instances of supernatural events freed from superstition and mythology, and, therefore, the criteria of reason are satisfied. Christianity is true. If a theologian rejects Christian evidences, this has nothing to do with their objectivity but is simply a comment on the elements of unbelief or misunderstanding in the mind of the theologian. Or, his rejection reflects the fact that the theologian is a victim of his own cultural climate and therefore does not give Christian evidences a fair evaluation.

This view is not free from some very serious objections. (1) Human sin blocks man's reason so that he either cannot see the supernatural for what it is or he rebels against it. He challenges the authenticity of the report of the supernatural, or he objects to its antiscientific character, or he classifies it with prescientific mythological thinking. (2) The concept that reason tests a revelation represents a modern way of understanding an ancient document and oversimplifies the very complex nature of the verification of theological beliefs or divine revelations.

The *Probabilists* (again my term) do not believe that Christian evidences can function as the gospel. The function of Christian evidences is to create a favorable attitude toward the Christian faith. This has been called historical faith. Historical faith is the bridge from unbelief to saving faith. Something must get a man moving in his thinking so that he will consider the gospel seriously. Christian evidences shows the measure of substance and reality to the Christian faith and sets the mind of the unbeliever in motion. Once historical faith is established there is a real possibility (but not a necessary consequence) that the sinner will put his faith in Christ.

This view is not essentially free from the objections to the first view although its claims are more modest. The most common objection is that it represents two-step evangelism. The first step is historical faith, and the second step is saving faith. But the problem still remains. Can historical faith really buck successfully the sinful disposition of man? As a matter of fact, only a very small percentage of Christian converts go through the process of moving from historical faith to saving faith.

The *Negativists* really see no apologetic value in Christian evidences. This is characteristic of Christian apologists with a strong philosophical approach. In some cases their preoccupation with philosophical apologetics is so great they simply omit any consideration of Christian evidences. Or, they may neglect Christian evidences on theoretical grounds. A man will believe in evidences only if on philosophical grounds he believes Christianity to be true. If he believes Christianity to be true on the basis of a philosophical apologetics, he then accepts Christian evidences as part of the biblical witness, but it does not really have an apologetic value or function for him.

Calvin's position. In *The Institutes of the Christian Religion,*[3] (bk. 1, chap. 7), Calvin affirms that only the Holy Spirit can bring a man from unbelief to faith and give him assurance, certainty, and conviction that the gospel is true. This proves, therefore, that the Holy Scripture in which the gospel is imbedded is true.

Chapter 8 is entitled "The Credibility of Scripture Sufficiently Proved, In So Far As Natural Reason Admits." Apologists have had a long battle over the meaning of this chapter. Some say that if chapter 7 is correct, then chapter 8 is inconsistent with chapter 7, and Calvin made an error to include it in his *Institutes.* Others argue that unless chapter 8 is added Calvin would not be able to defend himself against the charge of subjectivism (that is, resting his whole apologetics on the inward witness of the Spirit), and he would also be guilty of ignoring the evidential materials in the Scriptures themselves. I side with this second interpretation for the following reasons.

(1) I agree with Calvin that only the Holy Spirit is equal to man's sinfulness, and the Holy Spirit alone can break through that sinfulness with the gospel and the assurance of its truth. Chapter 7 must come before chapter 8.

(2) I agree with Calvin that Christian evidences will not impress a man in his sin since they are based on his ability to reason and think and evaluate correctly in his depravity. This is just not the case.

(3) I agree that chapter 8 belongs in the *Institutes* because it does

---

3. John Calvin, *Institutes of the Christian Religion*, vols. 20–21, ed. John T. McNiel, trans. Ford Lewis Battles (Philadelphia: Westminster Press, The Library of Christian Classics).

prevent Calvin from being charged with subjectivism; it does come to terms with the evidential materials in the Scriptures themselves (even though some of the topics Calvin appealed to we would not appeal to today) ; and it does shore up in its own way, and in its proper place, the veracity of Holy Scripture and the gospel it contains. Or, to put it otherwise, it does show that the God of Israel, and the God and Father of our Lord Jesus Christ, are not empty religious concepts or barren theological notions. This God does come into our time, our history, our space, our cosmos, and make a difference. Because God makes this difference, we know that we are believing truth and not fiction or mere religious philosophy.

BIBLIOGRAPHY

Books which enlarge the idea of Christian evidences and speak more of the action of God in history as the real demonstration of the reality of God are as follows (selected):

Barth, Karl. *Church Dogmatics* I/1–I/2. Translated by G. T. Thompson and Harold Knight. Edinburgh: T. & T. Clark, 1936, 1956. Barth speaks at great length of the signs of revelation, primarily the church and Holy Scripture but not limited to these, which are the historical indicia that God has given his revealed Word.

Casserly, J. V. *Toward a Theology of History.* New York: Holt, Rinehart, & Winston, 1965.

Connolly, James M. *Human History and the Word of God.* New York: Macmillan, 1965.

Filson, F. V. *The New Testament against Its Environment.* Naperville, Ill.: Allenson, 1950.

Pannenberg, Wolfhart, ed. *Revelation As History.* New York: Macmillan, 1968.

Wright, G. Ernest. *God Who Acts.* Naperville, Ill.: Allenson, 1952.

———. *The Old Testament against Its Environment.* Naperville, Ill.: Allenson, 1950.

IV

An Outline of a System
of Christian Apologetics (continued)

Section 7: Circle Three—Synoptic Vision

A certain unintended duplicity exists in every university in America. In some introductory course to a science, the scientific method is carefully explained to the student. The student is informed that when a projected hypothesis is confirmed by experimental results it stands as a verified hypothesis. This strict control on hypotheses eliminates the sloppy thinking of past generations and clears the mind of the current student from prejudices, emotions, sentiments, and hallowed traditions. When this takes place, the student has taken his first step toward becoming a real scholar and scientist.

He learns further to become rigorous about facts, data, mathematics, experimentation, verification, falsification, and all the other assumptions which are part of the scientific method. If he will follow such standard procedures, he can weed out or establish hypotheses through the processes of verification and falsification. Through this process our scientific knowledge grows and grows, and the apt student is a participant in it.

When the student advances in his studies, he learns the distressing fact that scientists following the same rigors of the scientific method espouse different theories. The most unusual example of this I have come across is Robert A. Harper's *Psychoanalysis and Psychotherapy: 36 Systems.*[1] How can scientists following the rigorous and vigorous scien-

---

1. Englewood Cliffs: Prentice-Hall, 1959.

tific methodology produce thirty-six different theories? And although the variations do not count up to thirty-six, certainly there are many alternate theories about historical knowledge, economics, and politics. How distressing to learn that experts who have devoted their entire lifetime to a given subject matter disagree!

How do we explain this phenomenon to the student when we have already indoctrinated him with the idea that vigorously controlled scientific experimentation leads to the truth? How do we explain to him that there are a number of books in the university's library which are devoted to setting forth alternate theories upon subject matters that on principle should be excluded if the scientific method were strictly followed?

Of course, the answer is that something has been left out in explaining the scientific method to the freshman. There is no question about the amount of truth in the scientific methodology in which he was instructed. The heart of the problem is that something has been left out of the neat steps given him in the so-called scientific method. What has been omitted?

A scientist or a scholar accepts some basic theory in his discipline certainly on so-called facts and verified theories. But facts and theories come in bits and pieces, whereas a science represents a whole scheme of things as does any theory. So added to the factual and verified materials is the perspective of the scientist. A theory "makes sense to him," or the theory "makes a meaningful pattern," or "things look right put together this way," or "that package looks like the right stuff," or "I'll buy that," or "now that picture is the real thing." This I call *synoptic vision*. Scholars who agree on particular facts disagree on larger theory because they have different synoptic visions.

For example, the most vigorous of philosophies is the so-called analytic philosophy, or linguistic philosophy, or verification philosophy. The usual basic refutation of this theory, the statement "Only those sentences are meaningful which as a matter of fact or in principle can be verified," is a sentence which cannot be verified. It is not a formal sentence that is consistent within a system of symbols; nor is it a material sentence affirming a status of affairs in the universe. But this does not really bother these philosophers. They say, "Grant us this principle, and we can make more sense out of philosophy than any other competing principle." In our language they adopt their system on the basis of synoptic vision and not because they have a complete system with no gaps, interstices, assumptions, or leaps of faith.

The genius of this movement of philosophy was Wittgenstein. He made the remark that once philosophy had done its work it would cease to exist. How can philosophy put itself out of business? The function of philosophy is to enable us to utter meaningful, and only meaningful, statements. At the present time we are uttering all kinds of mumbo jumbo. But when the day comes and we learn to speak perfectly from the logical point of view, we shall utter only meaningful statements. Philosophy has then fulfilled its task and will cease to exist. But what keeps Wittgenstein and his followers going, on the move, writing philosophy when the present state of affairs is so far removed from the anticipated goal? To me there is only one answer. Besides working with some version of the verification principle (unfortunately this philosophy has discovered that it cannot follow one theory of verification but has budded two or three others), these philosophers work with synoptic vision. They admit that they have unanswered problems and difficult situations where it is hard to imagine how the verification principle is applied and that very critical books have been written against their system. But they stick with analytic or linguistic philosophy because in spite of all problems and objections it still makes the most sense for them. In short, it is accepted on the basis of the kind of synoptic vision it gives the philosopher.

Because all sciences and other areas of learning are incomplete, they can only be rounded out by synoptic vision. In that the data is capable of a number of possible synoptic visions, at the present time scholars and experts do differ because they have different synoptic visions. This is why there exists in our universities the discrepancy between the very articulate way in which the scientific method is set forth as the gateway to knowledge and the fact that professors of equal competence in the same department have very sharp differences in basic theory.

In order to acquire a synoptic vision, the scholar looks over the whole field of his specialty. He tries to see it as a totality, a system, an organism, and not just a heap of facts. The term *vision* indicates that the scholar has left the criteria of sheer factual verification and is looking for a pattern, a configuration, a model, a picture, a complex diagrammatic chart by which he can synthesize his discipline into one unified theory or interpretation. That pattern or that picture which has the most appeal to him, that puts things together for him in the most meaningful way even with the lack of a great number of important data, is the one he chooses. That is his synoptic vision.

There are historical examples and similarities to what I call synoptic vision. Plato's dialectical method is similar to synoptic vision. That is, his posing of alternatives, running down the implications of these alternatives, the give and take among the debaters in the *Dialogues*, and choosing the best possible of alternatives is synoptic vision seen in its functional perspective.

Synoptic vision is similar to what the existentialists call decision. The person chooses that life style which in its totality is the authentic life style for him. Thus, the existential or authentic decision is not a piecemeal decision. It is a decision about the total scope or character or pattern of one's life. It is not based on sheer facts or verified data, but it has vision and imagination. It is a version of synoptic vision.

Synoptic vision parallels certain psychiatric theories. The psychiatrist tries to develop a theory of pathology that will account for all basic deviations from normal behavior. He grants that not nearly enough facts are in for any final, dogmatic position, but he has to work with some kind of coordinating theory. Therefore his working theory of pathology of the personality is his psychiatric synoptic vision.

One of the central theses of existential psychotherapy is that the psychologically sick person puts his whole world together the wrong way. It is not just a matter of a wrong type of reaction to a specific situation. The total way he sees reality and the total way he reacts to it is the total way in which he is sick. He is sick in his synoptic vision and therapy is to help him arrive at a healthy synoptic vision. The perfect example of this is the paranoiac person who has a completely systematized delusion of persecution. His synoptic vision systematically and infallibly distorts reality. He is not sick because he acts oddly in a few situations; his whole life is put together around a fantastically systematized falsification.

Kant had his version of synoptic vision. Kant did not believe that man was the recipient of bits of information from his senses which he stored in his memory and then at the necessary times was able to recall this information to make an act or decision. To Kant the mind unified, systematized, and synthesized experience into a world, and man lived and acted in this synthesized world. That synthesized world is man's synoptic vision.

This is the case with the Christian. He is convinced of the truth of his faith by the witness of the Spirit. He is convinced of the truth of his faith by the actions of the living God in the cosmos which makes a difference. And he is a Christian because he believes that the Christian faith gives him the most adequate synoptic vision there is with reference to man, humanity, the world, and God.

Like any other synoptic vision, the Christian's synoptic vision is composed of many elements. There are factual elements of all kinds such as biblical history, biblical geography, ancient history, comparative linguistics of ancient languages, and the critical study of documents. There are interpretative elements such as history and philosophy of history, the study of the history of philosophy, especially where it overlaps Christian topics, and the broader psychological understanding of man. There are personal elements such as one's conversion experience, one's prayer life, one's important spiritual decisions, one's experiences of common worship and fellowship, one's reading of Holy Scripture and theological literature. There are experiences of joy and depression, of freedom and guilt, of victory and defeat, of inspiration and temptation, of coldness of heart and spiritual renewal.

These synoptic visions are not identical with each Christian for there are both overlap and differences. The one thing that all Christians have in common is that their faith gives them the most satisfactory understanding of themselves, of God, of their relationship to God, of human history, and the place of the whole cosmos in human experience.

Yet the Christian does not believe that this synoptic vision is purely his own doing. Emil Brunner says that the Christian philosopher begins his philosophy from the perspective given to him by divine revelation. God's grace and God's salvation and God's revelation are all factors helping each Christian form his synoptic vision so that what he comes up with is not a matter of arbitrary choice. As a forgiven sinner man does not believe that it is his holiness or his learning or his cleverness that has put him at a point of advantage from which he forms his synoptic vision. It is a gift of grace.

Brunner has stated this another way: the Christian's subjectivity is that which is given to him by the Holy Spirit. Subjectivism is that which a man chooses and believes is right because he chose it. It is not adequately related to external criteria. But faith has to be subjective! It is personal commitment. It is the voluntary acceptance of a truth about God and a total way of living. Brunner's point is that the believer does not arrive at his subjectivism (his synoptic vision) on his own. There is an objectivity to it. That objectivity is that the Holy Spirit is God's agent in helping, aiding, guiding the Christian to the right faith, the right synoptic vision. So his faith is subjective (it is an internal matter of choice), but it is not subjectivism because the choice is not arbitrary. It is arrived at with the help of God's Spirit.

It is common knowledge among pastors that there is a great loss of young people from the church between the ages of eighteen and twenty-two. It is also proverbial that a number of college freshmen each year give up the Christian beliefs of their childhood and church. To be sure there are psychological and sociological factors at work as well as intellectual ones, but this loss of faith does come at this time of life. Frequently this is charged to the skeptical views of a professor, or the criticisms of Christianity in some particular textbook, or the general anti-Christian and antireligious mood that pervades both the business and the academic world. Getting down to the root of the matter, what is the real cause of this loss of faith?

I think the real reason is that the student received in church only bits of Christianity here and there. He knows some of the Old Testament stories and most of the incidents in the life of Christ. He has heard some elements of theology in the preaching service. But he never makes a synoptic vision out of all of this. His faith resembles a patchwork quilt.

Then the student enters college or engages in some other kind of exposure to alternate Christian views. He begins to take the patches and form a true synoptic vision. What he avoided while in high school and under the influence of the church he now undertakes. Since he did not do this in his younger years, he does it in college, business, or society. The Christian bag of scraps has lost its meaning and relevance. Scraps cannot compete with synoptic vision. So the young college student has not so much lost his faith as he has found a new, functional, operational, sensible synoptic vision which he did not forge while in church. He is done with Holy Scripture, Christ, the church, and salvation because now he has a synoptic vision which he never had in his youth.

The importance of synoptic vision to Christian faith is then of immense pastoral concern as well as apologetic concern. The final battles of life are over synoptic visions, or, in other language, they are ideological. The really great battles are for men's minds not men's territories.

Synoptic visions are not to be arbitrary choices but responsible choices. Some sort of specific criteria must be considered to help sort out synoptic visions and also to help support the Christian synoptic vision. Some of the elements which indicate a responsible synoptic vision are:

A responsible synoptic vision must have reckoned with a measure of factual support. The mere choosing of a synoptic vision does not make it true or free from measurement from some kind of criterion. A synoptic vision may be false as in the case of idolatry. Synoptic visions must show some interaction with concrete data or facts or the realities of the cosmos.

Suppose it were possible to write three novels in such a way that no clues in the character of the writing would give away the character of the book: (1) a novel of complete historical fiction; (2) a novel in which historical fact and fiction were woven together; and (3) a book of genuine history but cleverly written in the form of a novel. How could we separate them and classify them?

They could be classified by the character of their factual content. The novel of pure historical fiction could be detected because none of its facts could be verified; the historical novel could be detected because it was part fact and part fiction; and history in novel form could be detected because it was all fact and no fiction.

A synoptic vision must face a similar factual analysis or it is not a responsible synoptic vision. A synoptic vision with integrity has been honest with the facts.

The Christian synoptic vision is accepted in integrity and responsibility because it has come face to face with facts. In Scripture there are all kinds of facts—natural science, meteorology, geology, history, geography, natural history. Any recent dictionary of Holy Scripture, books on archeology or plants or animals of the Bible, biblical history, or biblical geography indicate the verification of literally hundreds of facts stated in Holy Scripture. In fact the Christian contention is that enough facts have come in to show that the Christian synoptic vision can be considered a responsible position to hold.

There cannot be complete, factual verification of Holy Scripture. Not all history has been recorded, and not all that has been recorded has been preserved. Scholars today do not know exactly what all the animals and plants mentioned in Holy Scripture refer to. Some statements about geographical matters in Scripture are still obscure.

The expression *archeology proves the Bible* is a poor one. The lay person takes it to mean that certain archeological information which concurs with certain biblical passages proves that the theology of Scripture is true. This is not the point. The point is that many matters of a factual character in Scripture have been directly or indirectly substantiated by archeological research. Certain factual elements in Holy Scripture have archeological support, but no proof of inspiration or divine revelation comes from archeology as archeology.

The apologist does not claim that every fact in Scripture is directly or indirectly verified. Furthermore, he admits that in some cases archeological research has created unexpected difficulties with the biblical text. But we are not discussing total verification or factual substantiation at all points. The question is: is there enough factual support from the study of archeology, ancient history, and geography to affirm that the

Christian synoptic vision is a responsible one at this level? Without listing the supportive materials which would run into the thousands of facts, the Christian apologist believes that his choice of the Christian synoptic vision is a responsible one when assessed from the standpoint of the amount of factual evidence that has gone into making the Christian choice.

To many critics of evangelical Christianity, the issue did not so much concern the correspondence of factual statements in the Scriptures with facts known by various kinds of biblical research. The primary issue was about biblical criticism which made it impossible from their perspective to maintain the evangelical attitude toward Scripture. The following is an oversimplification of the historical situation, but it sharpens up the focus of the integrity of Scripture and its theological validity.

On the one hand the staunch conservatives accepted the traditional views about the composition of the Scriptures to be true. That which was handed down through the centuries by Jews about the Old Testament and the Christians about the New Testament was taken at face value unless there were compelling reasons to do otherwise. From such a conservative view of matters of biblical introduction, a conservative biblical theology was constructed.

On the other hand the advanced liberal critic believed that all traditions had to be sifted to see what was historically valid within them. Furthermore, every book of the Bible had to undergo careful scrutiny to see if it was all that it was claimed to be by Jewish and Christian tradition. The result was a drastic new view of the status of Scripture generally tabbed higher criticism. Those who accepted higher criticism also believed that this was a summons to a new theology. The result was that the critical views of Scripture known as higher criticism and a liberal reinterpretation of Christianity went hand in hand.

A number of scholars in Europe, England, and America did not accept this either/or way of relating criticism and theology. They granted the right to the critic. As a human document the Scriptures had a historical side, and criticism had every right to explore the human and historical aspect of Scripture. But this did not challenge or deny the theological status of Holy Scripture. Its great truths were still the great truths of God. These scholars were called subsequently biblical realists. A German representative would be Kahler; a British representative, Denney; and an American representative, Briggs.

Some conservatives and some nonconservatives still see the issue very much as it was in the nineteenth century. Conservative biblical introduction is the necessary presumption of evangelical theology; the newer forms of biblical criticism require the formulation of a new kind of nonevangelical theology.

There are today a number of very able evangelicals whose position is approximately that of the biblical realists of the late nineteenth and early twentieth centuries. To them there is a reasonable, necessary, and valid critical approach to the Scriptures. Views are not necessarily true because there is a long tradition behind them or because they have existed for centuries without being challenged. We are in no position to pontificate on how God gave the Scriptures to the church.

There is a remarkable chapter in Helmut Thielecke's *Between Heaven and Earth* (chap. 2, "Historical Criticism of the Bible").[2] Thielecke shows on theological grounds that God treats men in honor and expects them to look at his Word critically. God does not insult our intelligence or suppress our curiosity or deny our need for knowledge. To honor God's Word the right way and to show the integrity of our faith, we must admit the legitimacy of biblical criticism. Thielecke makes it very clear that this defense of the right of biblical criticism is not based on prejudice or skepticism or in defense of academic freedom but on theology.

Furthermore, it was Machen, the intellectual leader of fundamentalism in the period of its greatest controversy with liberalism, who said of biblical criticism, "I have never been able to dismiss the 'higher critics' *en masse* with a few words of summary condemnation. Much deeper . . . lies the real refutation of this mighty attack upon the truth of our religion; *and we are not really doing our cause service by underestimating the power of the adversaries in the debate.*"[3]

Certainly an evangelical believes that there is a limit to criticism. A critical view of Scripture which makes any theory of inspiration or revelation impossible to defend, that destroys any notion of the final authority of Scripture and the essential concept of a canon, would of course be the end of evangelicalism. One cannot go the whole route with Bultmann and stay within an evangelical understanding of Scripture or theology. On the other hand, although Barth's position may seem too open-ended to some, there is a measure of truth in it, namely, that the notion of Scripture as the Word of God and the theology derived from the interpretation

---

2. Trans. John W. Doberstein (New York: Harper & Row, 1965).

3. Quoted in V. T. Ferm, *Contemporary American Theology*, 2d series (Freeport, N.Y.: Books for Libraries, 1932), 1:258, italics mine.

of this Scripture are not necessarily tied to certain critical viewpoints about Holy Scripture.

What has frequently been called the evangelical position is not really so but the assumption or a priori of some evangelical or group of evangelicals.

The Scriptures do have a human and historical side in their composition. We must be careful of making a priori judgments about what must have been the way Scriptures were written to protect their theological validity. We must grant facts when facts are known to be facts in biblical criticism. We recognize that certain kinds of criticism are destructive of the theological integrity of Scripture. But an open-minded, open-ended evangelical can interact intelligently with biblical criticism without impairing the theological integrity of the doctrines of inspiration, revelation, canon, or Holy Scripture. In short, evangelical apologetics is not of necessity bound to a stereotyped version of orthodox views of biblical criticism characteristic of the debates of the nineteenth century.

A responsible synoptic vision must have a measure of internal coherence. There are various ways in which propositions relate to each other. If two or more propositions do not contradict each other, they are in a state of coherence. If they assert divergent matters of fact, they are in a state of contradiction. They may be related other ways (conjunction, disjunction, etc.), but we are not concerned with these other relationships. A responsible synoptic vision has a high state of coherence among its propositions.

At this point a serious problem emerges. Theologians may agree that in matters of logic, science, history, or psychology the law of noncontradiction reigns supreme. But the subject matter of theology is so different, so peculiar, so mysterious, so transcendental that the usual canons of logic fail us. That theology is not to be completely controlled by the test of coherence is challenged on such following typical grounds:

(1) In that revelation comes from God we cannot grasp it all by ordinary logic, for by very reason of its origin it is partially out of our control. Theologians do not have enough data to determine how revealed dogmas cohere.

(2) God's thoughts differ from our thoughts, and God's ways are different from our ways. The divergence between the human and the divine is so great that it is foolish to test divine revelation and divine action by the human test of coherence.

(3) In that God is the mysterious God, he is beyond our logic. Mysteries cannot be reduced to rational formulations subjected to human,

rationalistic tests. Mysteries are to be received, believed, and adored.

(4) The language of revelation is different from ordinary language. Since it is oblique, or parabolic, or mythological, or odd, the usual tests of rational discourse cannot be applied.

(5) If God is transcendental, incomprehensible, and infinite, literal statements about God are not possible. God can be spoken of only paradoxically or dialectically (for every yes, there is a no; for every no there is a yes). The test of coherence is inadequate to test paradoxical or dialectical statements.

This problem is not new. For centuries theologians have tried to balance one set of affirmations in Scripture with others. Whether this literature actually used words like paradox or dialectical we do not know, but it used language that amounted to the same thing such as two lines parallel to us here meet in God's infinity. It is only since Kant, Hegel, and Kierkegaard that the newer logical terms became common theological words.

Other theologians have resorted to the principle of complimentarity. In atomic physics, particles act like waves in some experiments (passing a beam of particles through gold foil) or like bullets in other experiments (as in an x-ray). Instead of saying the statements are contradictory, the physicist says that in some experiments particles behave like waves and in other experiments they behave like individual specks. The principle of complimentarity means then that physics believes both concepts at once. It has been suggested that some of the major tensions or paradoxes in theology be understood by the principle of complimentarity. Through one slit we see God as absolute Lord, and through another we see the freedom of man. This relationship is one of complimentarity and not of contradiction or paradox. Hence the test of pure coherence fails to help in the context of complimentarity.

Holy Scripture itself admits that there is a problem such as we are now discussing. Paul calls the Incarnation a mystery (1 Tim. 3:16, RSV). He also says that God's actions in history are unsearchable and inscrutable (Rom. 11:33, RSV). Isaiah records that "For my thoughts are not your thoughts, neither are your ways my ways, says the Lord. For as the heavens are higher than the earth, so are my ways higher than your ways and my thoughts than your thoughts" (Isa. 55:8–9, RSV).

Such verses do not eliminate the test of coherence, but they set a limit to it. If all Scriptures contained material that was so completely different from man's thoughts, then the divine revelation would be incomprehensible; or it would take an unusual divine revelation for each person so that he might understand the mysteries. The large element in Scripture that is within man's grasp can be tested by coherence.

However, the issue has another angle. There is a difference between a mystery and a contradiction. If the law of coherence were to reveal great numbers of contradictions in Holy Scripture, then it would be difficult or impossible to defend Scripture as a divine revelation.

The principle of coherence is certainly used profusely by man. He uses it in science, in the court of law, in political debate, and in all areas of scholarship and research. One significant contradiction can bring a whole system down. When scholars reject such divergent systems as Marx's socialism or Mary Baker Eddy's Christian Science, the principle of coherence functions all the way through the refutation.

Part of the verification of the Christian faith is the large measure of coherence found within it. This does not mean there are no problems or difficulties. They are of all sorts. One passage seems to say something different from another passage—for example, the tension between Paul and James on works and justification. One passage may vary greatly from another passage in reporting the same event, a phenomenon very common in the synoptic Gospels. Or, the style of Greek in 1 Peter is very different from 2 Peter. But such kinds of problems beset any system, scientific as well as philosophical or theological. The Christian apologist knows that if he forsakes Christianity he is not going to find another system that is free from serious problems.

The Christian apologist is convinced that whatever internal troubles the Christian faith may have these troubles are not serious enough to cause him to reject the Christian faith. He believes that there is enough consistency in the scriptural record itself and in the main Christian doctrines to warrant responsible belief. This measure of coherence is then part of his belief in the truthfulness of the Christian revelation. The problem may also be viewed functionally or pragmatically. There is enough light in Scripture for faith in what God has done for man, what he is now doing in salvation and providence, and in what he promises man that man needs nothing more to live a godly, holy, devout life of faith. More light may satisfy more curiosity, but it would not materially add to what a Christian needs to know for living a consistent Christian life with a reasonable Christian hope.

Perfect consistency cannot be the claim of the apologist. The number of facts in Scripture are too many for any one person to sum up. Perhaps in the future by the use of computers the degree of consistency or coherence in Scripture may be very accurately assessed. But until that is possible, the Christian apologist believes that there is enough coherence in the Christian revelation to warrant responsible faith.

Involved in the problem of consistency is the unity of Scripture. Many modern scholars do not believe in a logical form of unity or consistency of Scripture. The unity of Scripture is located in its doctrine of God, or in its constancy of perspective about God and man, or in its fundamental theology, or in its Christological emphasis. There is much truth in this approach to the unity of Scripture. But such a view of the unity of Scripture must come to some terms, some reckoning, with the formal or logical sense of coherence or else the other kind of unity of Scripture is going to pull apart.

Kierkegaard attacked the idea of systematic unity when he attacked Hegel's system. The result has been a great measure of suspicion among theologians about system in theology. This is reinforced by the impact of existential thought on modern theology in which it is affirmed that systematic theology in the old sense is an impossibility. At this point two comments are noteworthy: (1) All such nonsystematic theologies do have a measure of system within themselves in that their particular doctrines do show some relatedness. (2) If any theological system clashes too violently with formal coherence, it will eventually collapse from an internal weakness or from attacks by critical philosophers.

Luther expressed the partial character of Holy Scripture and therefore of Christian theology when he spoke of the theology of the cross over against the theology of glory. He felt that the scholastics of the Roman Catholic church wrote their theology as if they were already in their glorified state and could see all things clearly and systematically. But can one handle the cross this way? Certainly not. The cross is so mysterious an event, so baffling an event from the human standpoint that we cannot describe it exhaustively by a series of propositions. The brokenness of the cross speaks of the brokenness of all our knowledge of God. Therefore, Christian theology ought to reflect this brokenness, and when it does, it is called the theology of the cross. As much as any person would want coherence and system in Christian theology, he must not avoid what Luther intended to say with his expression the *theology of the cross*.

Section 8: Degree of Verification

Part of the work of the scientist and therefore part of the scientific method is to state the degree of possible error the scientist is working with. Measurements are never perfect whether of length or weight or quantity. The scientist is able to state the percentage of error within which he works. The scientific law or theory may be put in symbolic form and give the impression that it represents a perfect transcript of reality. But when the experiments about the theory are performed, there is always a fuzzy edge to them. The theory may seem to be perfect with no remainder, but this is not true of the experiment.

A perfect map cannot be drawn because distances cannot be perfectly measured nor angles perfectly registered. Every true map has its error of enclosure. So the question comes to the Christian apologist: What degree of error of enclosure is he working with?

In more familiar terms the issue is to attempt to specify what kind or what degree of certainty characterizes a system of Christian apologetics. How sure are we of what we believe to be the sure truth?

Logicians divide this issue into two sections. The first is the kind of certainty that pertains to systems that are made up of pure symbols. Logic, mathematics, algebra, trigonometry, and geometry are pure symbolic systems. They can be put to use in a practical way in science, astronomy, surveying, etc., but their practical use does not negate their original symbolic form. In such a system a deduced theorem is rated as certain. There is no plus or minus. If the theorem is properly deduced according to the rules of the system, the theorem is true without any qualification. But this kind of certainty can be obtained only in abstract systems.

In the physical world of space, time, and objects a second kind of certainty is employed. Any theory of science, small or large, is a probability statement. The concept of probability is one of the most complex in modern philosophy of science, but these complications are not of immediate concern to us. In ordinary conversation the idea of probability is roughly equivalent to chance, but in science it means the degree of evidence for the verification of a theory. The very complex problem is how to formulate in a meaningful way the concept of degree of evidence. For example, after performing a certain experiment so many times and getting the same result, repeating the experiment a hundred more times does not really increase the certainty of the theory in the mind of the scientist. In the so-called crucial experiment just one experiment may convince the scientists of the truth of a theory. But solving this problem is not necessary for our purposes. Our only point is that when theories are propounded about the world of space, time, and objects they are probability statements in that these theories have only limited verification and do not have the status of a theorem in a system of pure symbols.

In view of the problem of certainty or probability or verification, what is the status of the Christian faith? What type of certainty does the theologian work with? What degree of certainty can a Christian hope to have? The apologists divide into such representative positions as follows:

(1) If the word *demonstrate* meant the same to Thomas Aquinas as it does to logicians today, then Thomas believed that he could demonstrate the existence of God and so have the same kind of certainty as modern logicians believe belongs only to purely symbolic systems. Or, if the existence of God can be shown to be a necessary proposition, the proof of the existence of God would have the rank of certainty. (However, the vast majority of non-Catholic theologians and philosophers do not believe that Thomas has demonstrated that God exists using the word *demonstrate* in its modern logical sense.)

(2) Some Protestant theologians believe that when a person believes the gospel God gives him as part of the very structure of the gospel a conviction of certainty. To such theologians it is blasphemous or heretical to say that God exists—probably; or, Christ is the Son of God—probably; or, Holy Scripture is God's Word—probably; or, God answers prayer—probably.

This view has some affinity with the view of Thomas, but it differs from Thomas in that it does not affirm the certain demonstration of Christian theology. It does affirm that the very nature of the Christian revelation carries with it the aura, the attitude, the presupposition that it is certainly true.

(3) Other theologians believe that when a man encounters the gospel or the kerygma he is so overpowered by the very reality of what he encounters that doubt is impossible. It was Kierkegaard who said that if a man could debate whether he loved Mary or Susan the man was not in love. When a man is in love with Mary or Susan (my names, not Kierkegaard's), it is impossible for him to weigh in his mind which one he really loves. So a person who has experienced Christ has had such a powerful existential experience that it is impossible for him seriously to debate comparative religions. If he can, he has really not experienced Christ existentially.

Very close to this idea are the opinions of men like Brunner and Bultmann, but most emphatically those of Bultmann. The existentially informed faith in the kerygma brings such a compelling conviction that

God is encountered that no conceivable kind of secondary data can be used to support faith. Christian faith is then known to be true with existential certitude.

(4) The best solution to this problem, however, seems to be in the distinction between certitude and certainty.

Certitude expresses a degree of psychological or spiritual persuasion. Certainty expresses the state of the evidence for a particular belief.

As applied to Christian apologetics and the certainty with which it is believed the following structure emerges:

(1) In view of the divine revelation in Scripture and the internal witness of the Holy Spirit, a Christian may have full spiritual certitude. He believes with full certitude that God is, that Christ is his Lord and Savior, that he is a child of God, etc. He does not add to these convictions the word *probably*.

(2) In that so much of the Christian faith is a matter of history, ordinary or sacred, the logical status of Christianity is that of probability. Historical facts cannot be known with full certainty. Therefore on its historical side Christianity can never be known with certainty (that is, as if it were a purely symbolic system; or, that it has a probability status of 1). But it can be known with a high degree of probability.

(3) The Christian apologist then says that spiritually, inwardly, convictionally he rests his faith in full certitude; in reference to the objective historical, factual, etc., basis of the Christian revelation, he believes with a high degree of probability.

Section 9: The Problem of Doubt

Holy Scripture itself raises the problem of doubt. This comes to the surface most clearly in the so-called depression psalms (for example, Ps. 73) where the psalmist is in great confusion over the manner in which God seems to be mismanaging the affairs in Israel. Habakkuk speaks up to God in an amazingly frank way about his spiritual confusion, perhaps the frankest in all of Scripture (Hab. 1:12–2:2). Even our Lord was tempted of Satan to doubt. The father of the epileptic child expressed the turmoil between faith and doubt when he said, "I believe; help my unbelief" (Mark 9:24, RSV). The flaming darts of Ephesians 6:16 (whereby ships were set on fire and burned to the water's edge) most likely refer to the doubts planted in Christians. Peter's roaring lion, the devil (1 Pet. 5:8), is in the business of doubt.

Temptation and doubt are not sins when they stand for a state of conflict within the believer. Doubt and temptation may lead to sin, but not necessarily. It must be conceded then in Christian apologetics that doubt is a normal element of Christian experience, and the verification of the faith does not put an end to doubt.

Luther said that the believer was attacked by temptation (*Versuchung*) and by assailment (*Anfechtung*). Although he can use the words synonymously there is a special importance to his concept of *Anfechtung*, "to assail, to attack."

According to Luther whenever a person puts faith in Christ he arouses the devil. The devil is losing part of his kingdom. He therefore assails or attacks the Christian to bring him into doubt, unbelief, and sin. Luther took the biblical statements about the devil both literally and seriously. The devil attacks believers, and therefore *Anfechtung* was part of genuine Christian experience.

There have been attempts to analyze Luther psychologically (for example, Erikson's *The Young Man Luther*). It is difficult to analyze dead people psychologically as it can be done only through the literature about them. But conceding the possibility that Luther had some sort of neurotic problem or Oedipal conflict with his father, this certainly is not the whole story, and Erikson must be commended for the number of times he makes reservations about his interpretation. But if Luther could speak for himself he would be inclined, if I read him right, to see more devil in his life than Freud. The years of depression he experienced had more theological elements in them than psychological.

Luther's doctrine of *Anfechtung*, "sin bravely," and his doctrine of "at the same time justified and a sinner" are of one piece. They reveal that the power of the Word of God and the power of the Holy Ghost are not strong enough to eliminate every doubt from Christian experience. Luther would say that without *Anfechtung* there is no real faith. The devil never fights for possession but only for the prospect of losing a possession. Doubt, temptation, and assailment are signs of faith. There is too much earthiness in Luther, the sense of the reality of the devil, and the realization of the power of sin yet abiding in a Christian for Luther to believe in a Pollyanna Christianity or any version of the victorious life.

Christian apologetics in agreement with Luther does not intend permanently to put the Christian outside the possibilities of doubt. Christian apologetics is not a complete prevention of doubt. Satan can shake up one's apologetics. On the human and psychological level the apologist reads all kinds of assaults on the Christian faith which may well assault his own faith. Therefore it must not be surmised that a thorough knowledge of Christian apologetics is theological insurance against *Anfechtung*. Christian apologetics may be a very excellent means of combating doubt, but by investigating the problematic character of elements of the Christian faith, the Christian may find himself in mental perplexities which he never knew existed until he undertook the burden of Christian faith.

BIBLIOGRAPHY

May, Rollo, ed. *Existential Psychology*. New York: Random House, 1961. May gives a bibliography of works on existential psychotherapy generally illustrating the thesis that neurosis is the result of the wrong way of putting one's whole life together. It is an existential default.

The theory that truth is a combination of logical consistency and conformity to fact was taught by Brightman, *A Philosophy of Religion*. New York: Prentice-Hall, 1940, and claimed by Carnell to be his own theory independent from any influence by Brightman. Carnell, Edward J. *Introduction to Christian Apologetics*. rev. ed. Grand Rapids: Eerdmans, 1955.

Whether there are different kinds of logic or reasoning is a matter of great contemporary debate. Much of this centers around Kierkegaard. Compare the following:

Clark, Gordon H. *Religion, Reason and Revelation*. Nutley, N.J.: Presbyterian and Reformed Publishing Co., 1961.

Foster, Michael B. *Mystery and Philosophy*. Naperville, Ill.: Allenson, 1957.

Hepburn, Ronald W. *Christianity and Paradox*. New York: Pegasus, 1969.

Kimpel, B. *Religious Faith, Language and Knowledge*. New York: Philosophical Library, 1952.

Polanyi, Michael. *Personal Knowledge*. Chicago: University of Chicago Press, 1958.

Sponheim, Paul. *Kierkegaard on Christ and Christian Coherence*. Edited by Jaroslav Pelikan. New York: Harper & Row, 1968.

Thomas, J. Heywood. *Subjectivity and Paradox*. New York: Fernhill House, 1957.

The classic on the unity of the Bible is still Rowley, Harold H. *The Unity of the Bible*. Philadelphia: Westminster, 1955. This work contains immense bibliographical materials. Recent works updating the discussion are Bright, John. *The Authority of the Old Testament*. Nashville: Abingdon, 1967, and Westermann, Claus, ed. *Essays on Old Testament Hermeneutics*. Richmond, Va.: John Knox Press, 1963.

Luther's theology of the cross and his concept of attack (*Anfechtung*) will be found discussed in:

Althaus, Paul. *The Theology of Martin Luther*. Philadelphia: Fortress Press, 1966.

Bornkamm, H. *The Heart of Reformation Faith*. New York: Harper & Row, 1965.

Kadai, Heino, ed. *Accents in Luther's Theology*. St. Louis: Concordia, 1967.

Meyer, Carl S., ed. *Luther for an Ecumenical Age*. St. Louis: Concordia, 1967.

V
The Theistic Proofs

Section 10: Preliminary Considerations

From a discussion of the general scheme of a Christian apologetics, we now turn to specific problems. It has been customary to assume that the proof of the existence of God is a necessary and major element in Christian apologetics. However, Tennant thinks that the proof for the existence of a soul is prior to proof for the existence of God.[1] Bluntly stated, his point is that if man is a creature without a soul the whole attempt to prove that God is, is an empty one. There could be a God who created only animals, but this idea cannot be taken seriously by Christians. To Tennant the uniqueness of man, namely, that he has a soul, is procedurally more fundamental than the proof of the existence of God.

Tennant's position is mentioned as a caution to those philosophers who might think that all Christians rest their case on the validity of the theistic proofs. There is an anticipation of Tennant in Descartes who philosophically sets out to prove that he exists before he gets around to proving that God exists. And there are existentialists who reverse Descartes: "I am, therefore I think." Such approaches also would put the existence of the peculiar character of man prior to the proof of God's existence.

In the apologetic system defended in the previous chapters, the existence of God is already proved. In Christian apologetics one attempts

---

1. F. R. Tennant, *Philosophical Theology*, 2 vols. (New York: Cambridge University Press, 1969).

the verification of the whole Christian system which includes the existence of God. This idea was not clearly articulated in the previous exposition, but the existence of God was included in the verification of the Christian faith.

Since, however, there are special problems associated with the proof of the existence of God, it must be treated as a separate topic. In the exposition that follows it must never be overlooked that the Christian sees the existence of God within the context of the three circles of verification which we drew and not as an isolated theological or philosophical problem. For the Christian the existence of God is never only a philosophical problem or only a narrow theological problem. The reality of God is bound up with the entire scope of Christian revelation, Christian redemption, and the Christian understanding of history.

According to Holy Scripture the living God is worshiped by man, his creation. Faith or belief in God without this worship, or this serving, or the kind of spirituality found in the psalms, is not faith in the biblical God. God, creation, man, and piety are strongly related in Scripture. Each implicates the other, and if one item is deleted, the biblical version of God's existence collapses. One cannot prove the existence of God and then walk away from God, at least not according to the biblical doctrine of God. Man as creature, man in the image of God worships and serves his God. This is not an option but an obligation. In Holy Scripture the reality of God and the worship of God are inseparable. If philosophers separate these two concepts, they may be talking about God, and they may be talking about him very learnedly and very seriously, but they are not talking about the God and Father of our Lord Jesus Christ. When this God is known, he is worshiped. That a philosopher may prove the existence of God and at the same time remain completely indifferent to this God is contrary to the biblical attitude about God. This point was emphasized by Calvin when he said in the very opening chapters of the *Institutes of the Christian Religion* that a knowledge of God always includes piety and without piety there is no real knowledge of God.

The men of Holy Scripture who believed in God walked with God, prayed to God, sacrificed to God, danced before God, and sang about God. They nurtured a personal spirituality as expressed in the phrase *to walk with God*, and they engaged in public worship, first in the tabernacle, later in the temple, and still later in the Christian churches.

To believe in God according to divine revelation means that the believer has, in modern language, a value system that is distinctly theistic and an ethical system grounded in the holy nature of God. It also means that the believer has certain attitudes such as trust, faith, love, and hope which are directed toward God and his fidelity.

The men of Holy Scripture also possessed a necessary historical dimension to their faith in God because the God of both Testaments is a God who promises things he shall do in the future. Hope was as essential to their belief in God as faith and trust. Expressed otherwise, the biblical idea of God looks backward to creation and forward to the consummation of all things and is thus an eschatological faith. God is the coming One.

Because of these kinds of relationships between God and the faithful in Holy Scripture, Holy Scripture never entertains a pantheism. Pantheism would be destructive of the kind of spirituality the God of Holy Scripture demands of man. Similarly the idea that God is dead or that God is the Ground of all Being is to be rejected as not expressing the kind of God revealed in Holy Scripture nor the relationships this God obtains with his creatures. Cultural analyses (God is dead) or philosophical assumptions (the Ground of all Being, Tillich) are not substitutes for the revelation of the living God in Scripture.

This brings us to the complications surrounding the word *proof*. For this reason the expression *theistic proofs* is ambiguous. There is no simple concept of proof by which all things are proved. The functional or operational or concrete expression of proof is governed by the subject matter that is being discussed. A theologian may have one concept of proof in mind when he thinks of the proof of the cell theory of life, and a very different concept of proof when he thinks of establishing the veracity of a good friend, and still another concept of proof when he thinks of the proof for the existence of God. The kind of proof with which an existentialist would defend his position is a very different kind of proof than that which Bertrand Russell would use in defending his system. Therefore a closer look must be taken at this word *proof*.

Some matters are proved by sensory experience. To prove that the American flag is red, white, and blue is to look at it. To prove that salt is salt, one tastes it. To prove something in logic, mathematics, or geometry is to show that the theorem (item to be proved) is consistent with the axioms of the particular system. To prove that a theory in science is true is a complicated matter, but as a rule of thumb we say a theory is true if it is experimentally demonstrated. To prove that there is such a thing as a mystical experience is to have one. Proving is not one simple, single operation but represents a whole battery of procedures.

What kind of procedure is required to prove that God exists?

Paul Tillich does not believe that God can be proved because God is not an object among other objects whose existence can be verified or falsified. God as the Ground of all Being is beyond proof. Thomas Huxley thought that empirical matters of science could be proved but that things metaphysical or religious could not be proved or disproved. So he claimed he was agnostic, meaning that some kinds of things are of such a nature that neither their existence nor nonexistence can be demonstrated, and God is in this class. William James thought that where typical metaphysical arguments for God failed, God could still be a reality to man because belief in God has a cash value or a pragmatic function.

Most philosophers of the twentieth century do not believe that the existence of God can be proved. Only matters of an empirical nature which are subject to experimentation can be proved. There is nothing empirical about God, so his existence is incapable of any kind of proof. This conviction is reinforced by showing all the logical fallacies in the traditional proofs for God's existence.

It has been customary to divide the theistic proofs into three divisions depending on the kind of proof appealed to.

A posteriori. There is some feature of the universe or cosmos that can be accounted for only on the presupposition that God exists. There are cues in the universe that can be framed into a theistic proof.

A priori. There is something about man that provides the basic clue that there is a God. God is an innate idea (something we are born with), or he sustains the moral law of the universe, or he is the source of all value. Or, he is the subject of a unique mystical or existential experience.

Revelational. God comes to man and makes himself known in a compelling way.

Section 11: The A Posteriori Proofs

This kind of proof presumes that there is an element or elements in the universe that can be explained or understood only on the basis of an action of God. It presumes that man has the rational power to detect such elements or factors and come to the correct conclusion, namely, God exists. This proof further presumes that even though man is a sinner his mind is not so clouded that he cannot see the cogency of the argument. Man needs no grace, no help from the Spirit, and no divine revelation to demonstrate this proof.

This proof presumes that the universe is not self-explanatory. There are factors in the universe that cannot be explained by recourse either to law or to chance. Only on the presupposition that God is and God acts can the total character of the universe be understood.

There are proofs for the existence of God scattered throughout Greek philosophical writings, but the most systematic expression of the reasons for believing in God come from Aristotle. These arguments were in turn adopted by Thomas Aquinas in the Middle Ages and were set forth in five different versions. Some philosophers speak of Thomas's five proofs and others of Thomas's one proof in five versions. Because Thomas put forth the proofs in such a clear and connected way, most discussions about a posteriori proofs for God's existence revolve around the expression given them by Thomas.

What is there, then, in the universe that requires the existence of God if we are properly to account for the totality of factors in the universe?

Motion. There is obviously motion in the universe. The word *motion* here means more than locomotion (change of place). It also refers to any process in which there is development, such as the growth of a plant. But something cannot move itself; it can be moved only by an external agent or force. An infinite regress of shoves or pushes is contradictory. So there must be a Being who while not moved himself gives the original push and also continues in time as the ultimate source of all motion. This Being is the Unmoved Mover or God.

Causation. Things happen in the universe because one thing causes something else. The billiard ball effect is going on all the time. Again, something cannot be its own cause, for cause and effect are two different things. An infinite regress of causes is contradictory. Therefore there is a Being who is not the result of a cause but the author of all causes, the First Cause, or the Uncaused Cause, or God.

Possibility and necessity. Things exist in a network of relationships. They can exist only in this network. Hence, each thing is a dependent being. But an infinite regress of dependencies is contradictory. There must then be a Being which is at the end of the line of all contingencies, the Being that is absolutely independent (that is, not contingent upon anything else), and that Being is God.

Gradation of being. The universe is a pyramid of beings at different levels of perfection. There is, for example, a continuum of creatures from worms or insects to man in an ever-increasing degree of perfection. Above man are the angels. But there must be the final Being, the Supreme Being, the Fullness of Perfection. And that Being is God.

Governance of the world. The world is composed of many systems of means and ends. But the universe itself cannot create its own systems of ends and means. That is, design in a universe must be the result of a Being outside the universe who bestows the patterns of means and ends in the universe. This Being is God. This is known more generally as the teleological argument or the argument from design.

The argument from design is as old as Socrates because original forms of it can be found in Socrates' biographer Xenophon (*Memorabilia*). In the history of Protestantism this argument was stated with remarkable clarity and logic by William Paley.

However, it was seriously attacked by Hume and Kant from the standpoint of its philosophical weaknesses. Kant affirmed that the most it could prove was that the universe had an architect. To convert the architect into God, a theologian would have to add the ontological argument.

Not only philosophers have attacked Thomas. Scientists claim that the design in the universe is appearance but not reality and make their appeal to Darwin or evolution. No doubt the hand is a marvel of engineering, and the eye a very complex technical piece of equipment. But hands and eyes are the products of millions of years of evolution. Small variations in primitive eyes and hands gave the creature a survival value. As the struggle for life continued, those creatures with better vision and better extremities survived. Today man has a marvelous hand and a marvelous eye that appear as if they were the work of a master engineer. In reality they are the end product of millions of years of positive mutations that gave the creatures additional survival powers. The argument from design collapses because the universe can account for itself at this point.

However, in the twentieth century the teleological argument has received two new kinds of defenders.

(1) Biologists have attempted to show that there isn't enough time for evolution to take place by purely natural or chance factors within the two billion years that life is supposed to have existed on the earth. They have stated how fantastic are the odds against all of this happening in the prescribed time. Perhaps something like fifty billion years would be required for evolution to occur by natural selection through chance or random mutation. For example, getting the right atoms together to form the basic molecule of protein, the fundamental keystone for all life, presents such an incredibly high figure for its occurrence that the production of such a molecule by pure chance or the principle of indifference (something can go one way as well as another with no predisposing factor present to cause it to prefer one way against another as in tossing a coin or rolling a dice) is impossible. Or, the possibility of a barrel of

dirt eventually mutating into a horse is $(10^3)^{10^4}$ which is a figure running into millions of zeros. On the basis of pure chance or random selection it is an impossibility so to produce a horse.[2]

This is not a new argument. In 1944, A. Cressy Morrison published a very popularly written book *Man Does Not Stand Alone*. On the first page of the book he indicates that the probability of drawing ten pennies out of one's pocket in the correct order (that is, each penny has a number on it from one to ten) is one in ten billion. The rest of the book shows that the universe is infinitely more complicated than ten numbered pennies and that for all the conditions for life to emerge and develop the probability is so utterly fantastic that it is unbelievable that life could occur by pure chance.[3]

In 1947, Lecomte Du Noüy published *Human Destiny*. Here the argument gets more technical. Du Noüy relies on the mathematics of Charles-Eugene Guye. The size of a universe adequate to possess the necessary factors to produce a protein molecule of two thousand atoms is one with a volume one sextillion, sextillion, sextillion times greater than the universe's dimensions as figured out by Einstein.[4]

Both of these men know that theoretically baboons could type out all the books in the British Museum or the Library of Congress. Or, theoretically a child could beat a chess genius in thirty-four moves. They also know that pulling ten pennies out of one's pocket in the right order is purely mathematical probability but that in the empirical world such large probabilities are fictional.

For example, what is the mathematical probability that Jones meets Smith at a football game? The population in America is now, in round figures, 220,000,000. The mathematical probability is then 1 out of 220,000,000. But most of Jones's friends live in his city where the game is played. Most of Jones's friends are of the age that likes to see football games. Jones's friends are for the most part men who like football. Most of Jones's friends graduated from the same university so they will all sit on the same side of the stadium. If it is the homecoming game, then even another factor is added. So empirically the chance of Jones meeting Smith is more like 1 to 10,000.

For reasons such as this (now in science, not football games), biolo-

---

2. See Errol E. Harris, *Foundations of Metaphysics in Science* (New York: Humanities Press, 1965), p. 233.

3. A. Cressy Morrison, *Man Does Not Stand Alone* (Old Tappan, N.J.: Revell, 1944).

4. Lecomte Du Noüy, *Human Destiny* (New York: David McKay, 1947).

gists do not like arguments from probability. In fact, they have an extreme distaste for them. That is not yet strong enough. Some biologists become violent and come near apoplexy in discussing the subject. Of course, Morrison is aware of this. In so many words he says that biologists will resist this kind of argument but given enough time the mathematics of the situation will force them to the wall and they will have to exchange their prejudices for the truth.

However, the biologist has the picture somewhat out of focus. Morrison, Du Noüy, and Guye know that they are working with the calculus of mathematics and that theoretically some very unusual things happen every day that from the standpoint of pure mathematical probability would have to be counted as miracles. Their idea is this: to set the outer limits of the situation. The question is then: how much can empirical factors (in the analogy of Jones meeting Smith at the football game) reduce pure mathematical probability? Perhaps if the reduction were 90 percent, the figure would still be too large to account for the phenomenon on the basis of chance empirically qualified. Or, the probability number might be increased. Perhaps we have underestimated the outer limits.

The point we are making is this: at the present time we have a problem that is controversial, and biologists cannot agree on a method of settling it as of the present. But there is a problem here. These probability figures are so fantastic they are not to be toyed with or tossed off as incidental. All that is being asked by the new cosmic teleologist is that the biologists and scientists show some basic intellectual honesty here which might require choking off some prejudices and biases and recognize a serious problem even though they might not like some of the answers being given to the problem.

(2) The attempt to show that God's creative activity is the only way of accounting for the design in a hand or a spinal cord or a brain (with its ten billion cells and one hundred billion glia or supporting cells) is known as organic teleology. As early as 1913, L. J. Henderson was working on a different kind of teleology.[5] This had to do with the nonorganic factors necessary for life to exist as we know it today. Since Henderson's time this school of thought has received the title cosmic teleology. A cosmic factor would be, for example, the distance of the earth from the sun. If the earth were too close, life would be impossible because the

---

5. See L. J. Henderson, *The Fitness of the Environment* (New York: Macmillan, 1913); and *The Order of Nature* (Cambridge: Harvard University Press, 1917).

temperature would be too hot; or, if the earth were too far away, the temperature would be too cool to support life as we know it. Henderson's books are filled with dozens upon dozens of cosmic factors that must be just right or life is impossible. Furthermore, these factors are not inter-related. The giraffe must grow a long neck to reach the leaves he feeds on; the deer must develop long, slender legs so he can outrun the carni-vore; the bird's beak must undergo change if it is to get at its special kind of norm. There is a correlation between the structures that the ani-mals develop and their possibility of survival.

In cosmic teleology no such connections exist. There is no necessary connection between the distance of the earth from the sun and the amount of nitrogen on the surface of the earth. There is no connection between the ratio of land to water on the earth and the fortunate tilt of the axis of the earth giving us the four seasons. If no connections exist as in organic teleology, and yet a fantastic number of such cosmic factors must exist for one single cell to emerge, then the most obvious answer is to say that God created it this way. To resort to probability or chance variation to produce these conditions calls for a greater miracle and a greater act of faith than believing in God.

Some biologists believe in biological teleology and cosmic teleology. They do not believe that Darwin's theory of evolution destroys biological teleology but fills in the details as to how it works. Further, the recent upsurge in process philosophy and theology is but modern reinforce-ment of cosmic teleology. In this regard Teilhard has almost been ele-vated to the rank of scientific saint. He weaves his theology and science into one great scheme of cosmic evolution, biological evolution, human evolution, and spiritual evolution.

Scientists are very inhospitable about this kind of thinking or reason-ing. Francis Bacon (1561–1626) was a great philosopher in Great Britain and gave much attention to the philosophy of science. One of his famous remarks was, "The research into final causes, like a virgin dedicated to God, is barren and produces nothing." By so speaking he ruled teleological explanations out of science, and his maxim has been one of the most cherished in the history of science. Some scientists have gone so far as to say that no matter what incredible or fantastic prob-ability figure is suggested for a given event occurring, they would re-main unimpressed. To them, final causes or teleological explanations are scientific virgins. And that is all they ever will be, and the most fan-tastic probability figure will never convert one of these virgins into a mother.

Again it must be said that science is at such a state of development that such issues cannot be settled. But a scientist ought to at least listen to somebody who stands outside the field of professional or academic science and tries to get a more synoptic view of the totality of human knowledge. And what he ought to hear is that that which may seem to him the most vigorous of scientific, objective, and aseptic conviction may be from an outsider's perspective an unsifted, uncriticized prejudice.

Section 12: The A Priori Proofs

An *a priori* proof is a proof that is based upon some aspect or facet or characteristic of man and not on any particular element in the cosmos. The notion of a priori means something inward and a posteriori suggests something outward. An a priori proof refers to something in man as the basis for proving the existence of God. Man's human nature contains a clue to the existence of a divine being.

There is no one single a priori proof. Many have been suggested in the history of philosophy and theology, and we shall take a look at some of these.

The existence of God is an innate idea. Something is innate if a person is born with it. The ability to remember is innate because children do not need to be taught how to remember or retain thoughts or experiences. Bouncing a ball is not an innate skill. The child has to learn to coordinate eye and muscle through many hundreds of attempts before he can skillfully bounce a ball.

In its simplest form, the argument is that every normal person is born with the idea of God implanted in his mind. As the baby grows to a child to a youth to a young adult, the idea of God becomes clearer and clearer. His experiences are richer, his powers of reason are greater, and his fund of knowledge is larger. From this comes the idea that there is a God. It may be very articulate or it may be hazy and at the edge of consciousness, but in critical experiences it may suddenly come alive. There are different versions of the innate idea of God. Some speak more of man having a religious nature or man having within himself a religious a priori (an ultimate religious faculty like thinking or willing). Calvin had the idea (which is also Augustine's) that God is continuously putting pressure on man. Man's sense of finitude, or man's sense of sinfulness, or man's sense of guilt, or man's positive gifts or attributes are ways in which God impresses himself upon man. Only sin prevents man from clearly seeing such matters as God's witness and therefore the witness of God to his existence.

The British philosopher, John Locke (1632–1704), vigorously attacked the notion of man having any kind of innate, a priori knowledge (*Essay Concerning Human Understanding*, 1690).

Some Calvinists, in contrast to Locke, have tried to show that man's fundamental decision about philosophy, whatever kind it be, is in the final analysis a religious decision. Man is a sinner and off the beam from his very first decision that reflects any kind of world interpretation that can be called religious or philosophical. The presupposition here is that in some way God is impressing his Being upon man so that if man does not go God's way he is responsible for the decision for going the wrong way.

Mysticism. All Christians are mystics in the broad sense that prayer and worship are directed toward an invisible God, and therefore the communication between God and man is hidden or mystical.

As a specific theory mysticism maintains that man is able to have a direct experience with God or a union with God which results in a profoundly ecstatic experience. If climbed, the so-called mystical ladder (with variations) leads to the mystical experience with God (for example, confession, contemplation, adoration). There is no automatic assurance that the mystical experience will follow, but it has, is, and will happen. If there is any such thing as objective proof in contrast to internal verification, it would be in the powers of love and holiness that the mystic has for the conduct of his life in society at the ordinary level of consciousness.

The union of God and man in mysticism is so unique, so overpowering, so incapable of doubt, that it self-validates the existence of God. This is based on the idea that there is an inside and an outside to man's experience. The outside is the world of the senses, of objects, of science, and of technology. Religiously it is a barren tract. The inside of man is his spirituality, his piety, and, therefore, the basis for the mystical experience.

The mystic may talk or write about his experience and give directions for the manner in which it is experienced, but the mystical experience as such is ineffable. It cannot be put into words that will adequately represent it. Only the mystical experience itself is self-validating. The mystic may witness to the mystical experience, but he cannot communicate it. Mysticism is based customarily on pantheistic or near pantheistic premises. However, there have been Muslim mystics, Jewish mystics, Roman Catholic mystics, and Protestant mystics. In the Christian religion the mystical experience is grounded in the concept of Christo-mysticism.

The classical exposition of mysticism is Evelyn Underhill's (1875–1941) *The Essentials of Mysticism* (1920).[6] Some Christian theologians have been skeptical or critical about mysticism on the grounds that it is inevitably pantheistic. Some maintain that Christian mysticism soon recognizes the validity of all mysticism, while others hold the opinion that mysticism as such is not taught in Holy Scripture. However, it must be admitted that 2 Corinthians 12:1–4 fits the criteria of a normative mystical experience; and by these criteria Paul did have a mystical experience. The customary rejoinder to this is that even if Paul had a mystical experience of the classical sort he never makes it a mandatory part, or even an important part, of Christian experience.

God is Truth. All men believe in some things as true. The agnostic and the skeptic are not exempt from this statement. To be an agnostic or a skeptic implies that one has enough truth in one area to believe that truth claims in other areas are false. If he believes in no religion because all the great religions contradict each other, he makes this judgment upon what he knows about comparative religions. One may base his rejection of religion or metaphysics on his knowledge of the limited, weak, finite, and restricted nature of man.

The radical doubter is in the same predicament. His denial is based upon a great deal of knowledge which, as far as he is concerned, does not warrant a metaphysical or religious belief.

The statement that God is a God of truth and the origin of all truth has a biblical foundation. The Old Testament identifies God as the God of light and truth and bears out the thesis that God is not only the true God but the God of truth.

The New Testament declares that Christ, the *Logos*, is the universal origin of life and light in man (John 1:4). In John 1:1, the Greek word *Logos* is translated *Word* and connotes rational speech in contrast to noise or sounds.

If God is the true God and the God of truth, then God is Truth. Philosophically speaking, this was a maxim in the Neoplatonic school and greatly influenced Augustine. The basic reasoning here is that truth is possible only as it is supported by Truth. The context of every single truth or little truth is the Truth. By definition this Truth is God; so the

---

6. New York: E. P. Dutton, 1930.

existence of truth implies the existence of Truth which in turn implies the existence of God and thereby is proof of the existence of God. This is the theory of truth propounded by Strong in his *Systematic Theology* which he labels as proof for the existence of God from the First Principle. This is also what theologians mean when they say that God gets in the way of the proof for the existence of God. Such a proof involves truth, but truth is possible only if there is Truth, and Truth is possible only as God is Truth. So, one has to presuppose the existence of God as the ground of truth in order to prove that God exists.

The ontological argument. This argument is rooted in Plato and Augustine but was formulated into a classic proof for God's existence by Anselm.

Some truths are contingent and some are necessary; or some sentences or propositions are contingent and some are necessary.

The affirmation that most barns in Sweden are red (because there is an abundance of soft red rock that can be used as the base of red paint) is a contingent sentence. The barns could have been painted yellow or green or blue. Their color is not a necessary.

The affirmation that ten plus ten is twenty is a necessary conclusion. The answer cannot be nineteen or twenty-one. The system of mathematics makes twenty the necessary answer.

Anselm attempted to formulate a proof of God that was necessary, namely, the very definition of God is such that God necessarily exists.

The essence of Anselm's ontological argument is that God is the highest possible Being we can think of and therefore the most perfect Being we can think of. But existence is a necessary property of a perfect Being. The thesis that God exists is then not a contingent statement (that is, it could be otherwise) but a necessary statement (because it can't be otherwise). The concept of the highest Being possible, the most perfect Being possible, by necessity includes the existence of such a Being.

To some this argument is a simple, obvious logical blunder. There is no connection between a perfect idea in a man's mind and the existence of that idea in the world. To others the ontological argument is the most profound proof of them all, for it is logically correct or in proper logical form and demonstrates that the existence of God is a necessary truth. John Hick[7] and Alvin Plantinga[8] have devoted entire books to

---

7. John H. Hick and Arthur C. McGill, eds., *The Many-Faced Argument* (New York: Macmillan, 1967).

8. Alvin Plantinga, ed., *The Ontological Argument* (New York: Doubleday, 1965).

the history of the argument as it has been debated through the centuries.

The real problem is to ascertain what kind of an argument it is. Is it an attempt to prove that God exists solely from pure rational premises free from any empirical consideration? Is it an effort to define and clarify the God of Holy Scriptures in philosophical terms? Is it the Apex of the pyramid of being in Platonic philosophy? Is it an innate idea that reaches fruition when man's mind moves from infancy to adulthood? In *The Existence of God* Norman Malcom gives a contemporary assessment of the argument.[9]

In my opinion the German historian of philosophy, Windelband, is correct in maintaining that the ontological argument is essentially an argument within Plato's philosophy. If Plato's philosophy is right, then there must be that Apex or Capstone Being that is the fullness of perfection, being, and reality. If there are no Platonic premises, then it is a clever maneuver in logic to so define God as to make his existence necessary and not contingent.

Recent literature seems to classify these proofs as clarifications of what faith in God means or what kind of God faith assents to. Since the rational argument appears to be defective, there is no proof in the traditional sense, but the proof functions as an instrument used to clarify the kind of person God is if a person happens to believe in God.

The argument from man's finitude. We determine how long things are and how much things weigh by the use of measurements. Such terms as *heavy* or *light* used about man do not say enough. Man has a sense of his finitude. According to Aristotle, man is in the circle of generation and corruption. He knows that he is a finite being. But what in his experience gives him this very deep sense of finitude? The answer is that man is constantly being confronted by Infinity, God. Though man is unaware of what is going on in his mind, God is continuously impressing man with His infinitude. This makes man very much aware of his finitude. So the sense of finitude itself is proof that an Infinite Being is the source of this sense of finitude.

The argument from blessedness. Philosophers of today are not impressed by the argument from finitude. They believe that man can realize his finitude by scientific knowledge. He does not need to take recourse to God to locate its origin. The same situation obtains for the argument from man's blessedness.

---

9. John H. Hick, ed., *The Existence of God* (New York: Macmillan, 1964), pp. 47 ff.

In the first pages of *The Confessions*, Augustine makes the point that man is restless until he rests in God. God has put eternity in man's heart, and man does not find real rest for his heart until he returns to God. Our very hunger for blessedness is a divinely given hunger and therefore an indirect proof that there is a God. Thomas Aquinas said that man has a vague longing for blessedness. The counterpart of this is that God is man's beatitude. But it was too vague to serve as a proof.

The argument from perception. Before the days of modern psychology the act of perceiving (by which philosophers meant that process by which the senses reported to the mind) was considered a mental act. A log burning in the fireplace was a physical event. But seeing the log burning was a mental event. The sort of things that go on when a log burns are of a very different order than the sort of things that go on when one perceives the log burning.

The average person probably accepts the chain theory of perception. The burning of the log produces heat which in turn produces light waves. These light waves impinge on the eye, and from the eye, nerves impress the light waves upon the mind. Hence, there is a chain of events from the oxidation of the carbon in the wood to the perception in the mind.

Bishop Berkeley (1685–1753), a very important modern philosopher (*Principles of Human Knowledge,* 1710), challenged this chain theory of perception. This theory presupposes that the burning log (our illustration) is a physical event which gives rise to a perception (a mental event). It seemed impossible to Bishop Berkeley that a physical event could cause a mental event. Therefore, he felt that philosophers could not appeal to matter as the source of their perceptions.

On the other hand, man doesn't create his own perceptions. They are given to him. I cannot decide whether I want to see a burning log or not. Something external to me must be the source of my perception of the burning log. If perceptions are mental (as understood in those days), then my perceptions must have a mental origin, and further an origin that does not give me perceptions helter-skelter but universally and uniformly in a way that demonstrates that I exist in an orderly cosmos which I share with my fellow-man. The only answer to this problem is God. God is a mental Person. God can give mental perceptions to my mind. Coming from God, these perceptions follow laws and form a universal system. Hence, the simple fact of perception proves that God is, for that is the only rational basis that can explain man's perceptions.

It has been said (although Berkeley did not put it this way) that

Berkeley's proof for the existence of God is the shortest in the history of philosophy: "I perceive, therefore God exists." We know a great deal more about perception and the brain now than was known during Berkeley's time, but in some ways this knowledge has increased the problem rather than solving it. The dilemma involves the fact that our understanding of the ways in which nerves transmit sensory materials doesn't jibe with the degree of clarity with which objects are perceived. We are still unable to show how a nerve impulse, basically an electrical discharge, can undergo transubstantiation in the brain and become a very complex perception.

The existential proof. Much existential philosophy has found its way into modern theology. Existentialism repudiates most of the traditional approaches to philosophy as well as theology. Existential theology denies the use of traditional rationalistic proofs for the existence of God. The existential theologian concurs that these proofs are more useful as a means of clarifying what we mean by the word *God* than proofs that he exists.

God as subject, God as transcendental, God as over against man (in an existential not spatial sense), God as sovereign or God as Lord (not in the traditional Calvinistic sense, but in the sense that God is not at our disposal) can only be known as God speaks to us or addresses us and summons us to decision. What he speaks is traditionally known as the gospel, but the word *kerygma* is more frequently used than *gospel* to indicate the existential character of this speaking.

The kerygma is God's declaration of his love, his forgiveness, his justification of man. This is the event and meaning of the cross and of the Easter faith. Nonexistential matters are settled by the typical means that scholars use to determine the truth or falsity of a statement. But an existential matter, the kerygma in particular, is something declared. It is spoken or preached. In the kerygma man is challenged to decision (or traditionally to faith). The kerygma addresses man, and man can respond to the kerygma only by decision for or by rejection. The truth of the kerygma cannot be settled by the usual or typical or scientific or historical methods. A kerygma can only be decided for.

In terms of theistic proof, God proves himself in the kerygma. When a man decides for God in terms of the kerygma, he knows God is. No historical argument, no philosophical argument, no scheme of Christian evidences are necessary to shore up his faith in God or authenticate his act of decision. A theologian should not really speak of the proof of the existence of God. To do so suggests a nonkerygmatic, nonexistential understanding of the Christian faith. The experience of the kerygma is self-authenticating and any effort to add to its integrity is a betrayal of the self-authenticating character of the experience of the kerygma. God is known existentially, vitally, really in the kerygma through decision (or through faith), or he is not known at all.

BIBLIOGRAPHY

For all the recent technical problems, logical objections, about the theistic proofs see:

Ayer, Alfred J. *Language, Truth and Logic*. Magnolia, Mass.: Peter Smith, 1946.

Blackstone, W. *The Problem of Religious Knowledge*. Englewood Cliffs: Prentice-Hall, 1963.

Burrill, Donald R., ed. *Cosmological Arguments*. New York: Doubleday.

Flew, A. G., and MacIntyre, A. *New Essays in Philosophical Theology*. New York: Macmillan, 1964.

Herrlin, O. *The Ontological Proof*. Leipzig: Otto Harrassowitz, 1950.

Hick, John H., ed. *The Existence of God*. New York: Macmillan, 1964.

Hick, John H., and McGill, Arthur C., eds. *The Many-Faced Argument*. New York: Macmillan, 1967.

McIntyre, John. *St. Anselm and His Critics*. New York: Hillary House, 1954.

Matson, Wallace I. *The Existence of God*. Ithaca, New York: Cornell University Press, 1965.

Plantinga, Alvin. *God and Other Minds*. Ithaca, N.Y.: Cornell University Press, 1967.

Plantinga, Alvin, ed. *The Ontological Argument*. New York: Doubleday, 1965.

This bibliography is intended to be the basic bibliography for all the chapters following on the problem of the existence of God.

VI
Typical Objections
to the Theistic Proofs

Section 13: The Present Status of the Theistic Proofs

Roman Catholicism has taught that the existence of God can be demonstrated by natural reason (the a posteriori ones being the only valid proofs). When Abbé Bautain declared that God is known only by faith and not by proofs, he was compelled to recant and confess that God's existence could be demonstrated by the light of natural reason (in 1835). Since Abbé Bautain was influenced by Kant, this was, in a sense, the Roman Catholic assessment of Kant's refutation of the theistic proofs.

In general, existentialism has not been viewed favorably by the papacy, and the encyclical *Humani Generis* (1950) adversely judged some of the current versions of existentialism. But existentialism, as well as phenomenology, seems to be coming into the Roman Catholic church through the back door. It is possible that the continued ferment within the Roman Catholic church will provide an atmosphere in which the strong Thomistic attitude toward the proofs for the existence of God will undergo modification, and it is even possible that permission may be granted to resort to alternate proofs. Already there is evidence that Roman Catholic theologians are seeing the theistic proofs in the wider context of revelation, philosophy, and experience and therefore do not see them primarily as solid, rationalistic, unequivocal proofs for God's existence.

In the nineteenth and twentieth centuries some theologians who were aware of Kant's criticism of the theistic proofs presented the proofs in a different manner. They described their proofs as evidential and did not consider them to be formal or logically compelling proofs. Their purpose was to present some sort of partial evidence for God's existence which if reinforced by moral convictions did assure one that God existed. Whether or not there is merit in this approach is debated even today. However, modern philosophers maintain that a wrong argument cannot be saved by recourse to moral support.

Historically the attack on the whole Christian system at an acute philosophical level was initiated by David Hume (1711–76). He in turn aroused the German philosopher Kant (1724–1804) who had accepted the traditional Christian philosophical apologetic of his times (principally after Christian Wolff, 1679–1754). Hume turned Kant's mind in a critical direction, and as a result Kant produced the famous *Critique of Pure Reason* (1787). In this work Kant demolished to the satisfaction of the vast majority of philosophers the traditional proofs for the existence of God by showing the logical inconsistencies within the argumentations.

Actually Kant did not need to take the space to refute the arguments for God's existence because the very structure of the *Critique of Pure Reason* made a statement such as *God exists* impossible. But Kant added insult to injury by picking out the logical flaws in the arguments. Philosophers ever since have considered these pages in Kant to contain the classical demolition of the theistic proofs. Hume had predicted the modern mood in a famous statement in *An Enquiry Concerning Human Understanding.*

> When we run over libraries, persuaded of these principles, what havoc must we make? If we take in our hand any volume—of divine or school of metaphysics for instance—let us ask, *Does it contain any abstract reasoning concerning quantity or number?* No. *Does it contain any experimental reasoning concerning matter of fact and existence?* No. Commit it then to the flames for it can contain nothing but sophistry and illusion.[1]

The number of objections to the theistic proofs has grown considerably since the time of Hume and Kant. This period (the eighteenth century) in Western philosophy was characterized by vigorous scrutiny of religion in general and Christianity in particular. Since the philosophy

---

1. David Hume, *Theory of Knowledge* (London: Thomas Nelson, 1951), p. 172. Italics are his.

of this period is very important for the development of philosophical theology and philosophy of religion in the twentieth century, the reader's attention is directed to James Collins's *Emergence of Philosophy of Religion.*[2]

Following is a typical list of criticisms of the theistic proofs, including those of Kant and Hume.

The proofs don't prove enough. A philosopher or theologian may not invoke a cause greater than the effect. If an argument is made for the existence of God from the cosmos, the argument for God's existence is drawn from a finite entity, the cosmos. All the cosmological argument, for example, could prove was a finite God, that is, a God just big enough to create a finite cosmos.

In this connection Kant argued that all the cosmological arguments presume the ontological argument which speaks of the kind of infinite God theologians demand. But if the ontological argument is invalid, all the proofs which presume it are defective.

With reference to the teleological argument, Kant said that it only argued for a divine architect and not for an infinite God.

The proofs are overburdened with logical difficulties. In its simplest form the ontological argument seems to assert that an idea of a perfect object means that the perfect object exists. Aguanilo, the foil in the dialogue of Anselm about the existence of God, said that the idea of a perfect island didn't make the island exist. In modern times Kant remarked the fact that he thought that he had one hundred perfect dollars in his pocket did not necessarily mean that he would find them if he put his hand in his pocket. One cannot go from an idea in the mind to reality.

This was in part a misunderstanding of Anselm (whose argument concerns the most perfect being one can think of rather than the perfect idea of any object), but it is also based on Kant's idea of existence. In Kant's thinking, for an object to exist it must be located in space and time and have properties. Another way of putting it is to state that existence is not a property of an object. God, of course, does not meet Kant's definition of existence, and, therefore, in terms of Kant's *Critique of Pure Reason*, God does not exist.

Thomas's five arguments are based on the idea that an infinite regress is impossible. Modern logicians to the contrary can cite a number of infinite regresses. For example, the number of fractions between two

2. New Haven, Conn.: Yale University Press, 1967.

and three is infinite. Or, the number of real numbers is infinite.

Thomas's arguments are based on propositions about nature being formulated exclusively in terms of causality. Modern logicians believe that statements about nature can be made without the use of causal language. For example, one can write, "if p, then q."

Physicists may claim that modern scientific laws are probability statements and not causal statements. For example, if a beam of atomic particles is passed through some gold foil, an x-ray of the effect will be one of concentric circles. We cannot take particle A in the beam of particles and predict where it will appear in the x-ray. The scientist can only give the percentages of distribution among the rings. Thus, the form of the law is statistical and not causal.

All proofs for the existence of God based on the principle of causation are now either suspect or invalid.

Modern logicians point out that in the arguments for the existence of God terms switch meanings making the argument invalid. The statement *heat causes water to boil* has grammatically the same form as the statement *God causes the universe to exist.* But a scientist has some idea of cause when he thinks of a gas flame causing a beaker of water to boil; however he has no idea what the word *cause* means when a theologian says that God causes the universe to exist. With the subtle switch in meaning of the word *cause* in the two sentences, the argument is made ambiguous and therefore inconclusive.

A whole new chapter in the logical problems of the theistic proofs was opened by Antony Flew's essay "Theology and Falsification" in *New Essays in Philosophical Theology.*[3] He said in effect that theists would not give a criterion or criteria whereby they would give up their belief in God. In logic a proposition that is true no matter what the conditions are is no proposition at all. So if theists state that they can believe in God no matter what happens in the universe then their belief is meaningless. It contains no criterion for its falsification. In this same connection, Flew said that theistic faith died the death of a thousand qualifications. The literature this one essay provoked is enormous in that it opened up a whole new nest of logical problems with reference to the theistic proofs.[4]

Another logical attack is that Thomas's proofs are really more in the nature of comments than vigorously thought-out proofs if checked out

---

3. London: SCM Press, 1955.
4. See articles in *Religious Studies*, October 1969.

by modern logical theory. Most philosophers in the analytic tradition would believe that this is the logical status of most talk about the existence of God by theologians.

The existence of God is not verifiable. Auguste Comte (1798–1857) is the reputed founder of sociology. He theorized that mankind went through three stages of philosophical development. First, man explained things religiously. Eventually religious explanations did not satisfy, and man began to explain things metaphysically. But this too proved inadequate. Third and finally man explained things scientifically. The French word *positif* means in one sense that which can be demonstrated by science in contrast to speculation. Comte is also the founder of *positivism*, the philosophy that claims that only really hard, substantial knowledge is scientific. The third state of man's development is that of positivism or scientism in which God is dropped out of man's beliefs.

A very gifted Austrian scientist and philosopher of science, Ernst Mach (1838–1916), is the source of the modern impulse of positivism. He read widely in empirical philosophy although I could find no connection between him and Comte. But the spirit of Mach came to life in Vienna in the famous Vienna circle. The public name of this circle was the Ernst Mach Association.

These men attempted to reformulate the whole task of philosophy in light of modern developments in logic, mathematics, and science. Their approach has been called logical positivism, logical empiricism, the linguistic school, and analytic philosophy. Due to the political turmoil of the 1930s most of these men migrated to England and America. Wittgenstein was considered the genius of the movement and his work *Tractatus Logico-philosophicus* (1922), its Bible.[5]

This movement has also been known as the verification school because it claimed that the meaning of a sentence was the manner in which it could be verified. If a sentence can be verified or falsified, it is a meaningful sentence. The verification need not be possible at the time, but in principle the sentence must be verifiable. *Grass is green* is a meaningful sentence because by looking at grass I see that its color is green. *Grass is scarlet* is meaningful but false because I can look at the grass (hence, I can do something about the sentence); but I don't see the color scarlet, so it is a false sentence. If no means of verification or falsification can be specified, the sentence is meaningless or nonsense.

---

5. Ludwig Wittgenstein, *Tractatus Logico-philosophicus*, trans. D. F. Pears and B. F. McGuiness (New York: Humanities Press, 1922).

Poetic sentences, ethical sentences, and theological sentences can state no means for their verification. They are not then false because false sentences can be meaningful if they can be checked out. Such sentences are rather senseless or meaningless because no possible program for their verification can be suggested. All theistic proofs are then considered meaningless or senseless because they cannot be stated in such a way that they can be verified.

The purpose of this short chapter has been to indicate in a general way how most modern philosophers look at the theistic proofs. There has been no attempt to evaluate these objections critically, but the matter will be discussed more in a subsequent chapter. For example, there are a number of British and American theologians who accept the general schema or system of analytic philosophy and claim that they can restate the character of Christian theology and the reasons for believing in the Christian faith operating with analytic philosophy. There are also some very able philosophers and theologians who state that for exterior matters they follow analytic philosophy and for interior matters (their Christian faith) they follow existentialism. This is an odd marriage, but it does exist; and for some keen minds, it is a viable solution to the problem.

BIBLIOGRAPHY

Out of the literature of the attempt to correlate the new analytic school and theology, I list the following books. They not only give the basic philosophy of this new school of analytic philosophy and so act as introductory guides to it, but they contain all the important references to the relevant literature.

Blackstone, W. T. *The Problem of Religious Knowledge.* Englewood Cliffs: Prentice-Hall, 1963.
Ferré, Frederick. *Language, Logic, and God.* New York: Harper & Row, 1961.
Gilkey, Langdon. *Naming the Whirlwind: The Renewal of God-Language.* Indianapolis: Bobbs-Merrill, 1969.
High, Dallas M. *Language, Persons, and Belief.* New York: Oxford University Press, 1967.
MacQuarrie, John. *God-Talk.* New York: Harper & Row, 1967.

VII
Theistic Proofs
and the Biblical Perspective

Section 14: The Important Stance

There is no formal proof of the existence of God in Holy Scripture. This means that the Bible contains no logically organized proof in some structure like a syllogism. The first man in the history of theology or philosophy who attempted to state the case for the existence of God in logical form was Aristotle. He in turn inspired Thomas Aquinas to develop his famous five proofs. But nowhere in Scripture is this kind of logical formulation for the existence of God to be found.

In the past, theologians have felt that certain Scriptures, though not formally organized proofs, virtually amounted to the same thing. These Scriptures are:

"Ever since the creation of the world his invisible nature, namely, his eternal power and deity, has been clearly perceived in the things that have been made" (Rom. 1:20, RSV). This verse was used by the theologians of the Middle Ages more than any other verse in the entire Scriptures.

"The heavens are telling the glory of God; and the firmament proclaims his handiwork" (Ps. 19:1, RSV).

"That they [the Gentile world] should seek God, in the hope that they might feel after him and find him" (Acts 17:27, RSV, part of Paul's famous Mars Hill address).

Two things, however, must be stressed at this point. (1) In form these verses are not typical, logical, organized proofs for God's existence and are not to be taken as short abbreviations of the same. (2) The scholastics did not make the later differentiation between general and special revelation in the crisp and important way the Reformers did; nor did they weigh as they should have the effects of sin upon the reasoning of man. The Reformers took off in an entirely different direction about the existence of God from the scholastics even though ironically not too long after the Reformers' deaths there was a Protestant revival of Aristotelian philosophy.

The whole weight of the biblical view of God is in another direction. Scripture is not a record of how man finds God but how God finds man. The point of departure in Scripture is not how man infers or proves that God exists by either a logically organized proof or an unusual experience but that it is God who breaks into man and lets himself be known. Hence, the key expression in Holy Scripture would not be *proof of the existence of God* but *the true knowledge of God* or *the reality of God*. The stance of Scripture is not that God's existence is formally substantiated by logically connected propositions (a sorites) but that God establishes his reality with man, that he gives man a knowledge of himself that is valid through acts of revelation and redemption. This kind of approach to the existence of God has the following characteristics.

It is a spiritual knowledge of God. Kierkegaard pointed out with great emphasis that the purely rational apprehension of something does not change the person who makes the rational apprehension. A man may be the world's greatest mathematician, and yet his personal life may be depraved, wicked, and spiritually empty. According to Kierkegaard, to believe in God is to undergo a major spiritual transformation; and without this transformation, there is only paganism. By the word *paganism* Kierkegaard meant a belief in God that called for no personal, spiritual regeneration.

A similar idea is found in Calvin. Calvin taught that a knowledge of God included piety, and to believe in God without piety is mockery. This would be like a soldier who never saluted a superior officer, never followed the orders of the day, and never kept military regulations. Though he might wear a uniform, he would certainly not be a soldier. Belief in God that produces no tangible piety is not biblical faith in God. True faith produces true piety—prayer, thanksgiving, worship, adoration, repentance, moral rectitude, attendance at the sacraments, etc. Philosophical proofs which deal with philosophical concepts but are utterly devoid of piety or utterly incapable of producing piety are talking about some God, but not the God of Holy Scripture.

Both Kierkegaard and Calvin are expressing ideas found in Holy Scripture itself. The psalms, as a case in point, cannot speak of God without speaking of trust in God, the fear of God, faith in God, dependence upon God, the worship of God, etc. The Old Testament expression *to serve God* means not just the conviction that God is, but that God is to be worshiped, honored, obeyed, and trusted. Proof of the existence of God without serving God would have been an impossibility for an Israelite believer.

Or take the important dictum "You shall be holy, for I am holy" (1 Pet. 1:16 with Lev. 11:44–45, RSV). Those who believe in God must reflect in their lives some of the moral perfection of God. To believe in the God of Holy Scripture without having in one's life some of the holiness of God is simply not to believe in the God of Holy Scripture. Philosophers and theologians may speak abstractly of God in his holiness, but without his demand of holiness in them that fear him, they are not speaking of the biblical God.

It is a gracious knowledge of God. The grace of God in its most general sense means that in the divine-human relationship God moves first. And if God moves first, he moves from considerations within his own being and not from considerations in the creature. In this sense creation is an act of grace, for God was not compelled to create. Salvation is of grace for it was God's immeasurable love that moved him to save man. Revelation is of grace, for revelation is the Word given to man who has not asked for it.

Hence, God coming to man, God breaking into man's cosmos, God breaking into man's horizon, God coming to man and making his reality and his knowledge known, is an act of grace. The traditional theistic proofs are strangers to the concept of grace as being the heart of the verification of the reality of God.

Since man's knowledge of God is founded on grace, believers are not smarter than nonbelievers, they are not more informed than nonbelievers, and they are not morally superior to nonbelievers. An event of grace rests upon the goodness of God and not on any quality within believers. This throws light on the "washerwoman versus the professor" discussion. How is it that a very ignorant person doing a menial task in life, totally ignorant of the liberal arts, the humanities, philosophy and comparative religions, has a simple, convincing faith and trust in God, and the professional scholar is five thumbs about this issue, filled with uncertainties and questions?

If the knowledge of God and the reality of God is of grace, then the washerwoman has a genuine spiritual certainty because she does not have to rely on her qualifications or learning but on God's action in her heart through the Spirit. If the professor has no such experience of the grace of God, then the theistic proofs are to him five thumbs and he gets caught in the well-known disease of the paralysis of analysis.

Christians who claim such a sure knowledge of God are the first to disclaim any kind of superiority. What spiritual certitude they have, they have by God's grace, and in grace there is no room for boasting (compare Rom. 3:27 ff.).

It is an objective knowledge of God. Modern secularized man is not necessarily intolerant with religion. However he sees religion as one's personal faith, an intellectual or an emotionally dictated need. Everyone has a right to his own religion, for it is solely a matter of faith or personal conviction and is not really debatable.

Such thinking violently conflicts with the biblical revelation. The true religion of God is "out there" as much as atoms, chairs, and planets. Its reception may call for something very important "in here" so that it is not completely on the same order as external objects. But in its essential character God's truth is objective, "out there," like the rest of the objects of human experience.

In Exodus 3:14 God says his name is "I AM WHO I AM" or "I will be what I will be." This is enormously important for the biblical understanding of the reality of God. God as the living God, as the real God, is not shown to be such in formal proofs, logical deductions, empirical inferences. He is known in the history he creates. By deliverance from Egypt, by the providential journey in the Wilderness of Zin, and by the occupation of the land of Abrahamic promise, God will be known as the living and true God.

Consider the difference between knowing a person on first impression and knowing a person through years of experience. Some people build their success on their ability to make a good first impression—the smile, the face, the curly hair, the interesting mannerisms. Yet when they are known through many experiences, their inherent superficiality or mediocrity may become known. On the contrary, a person whose first impression is very unassuming may show through the years that he is a very remarkable human being.

God does not prove himself to exist on the basis of a first impression or on the basis of an apparently airtight logical argument. Through many experiences, Israel would really come to know the Lord. Through many divine revelations, many divine providences, many divine miracles, many theophanies Israel would arrive at an immovable conviction of the reality of God, of God as the living Lord.

Therefore the philosophical approach to the existence of God and the biblical approach to the reality of the living God are fundamentally and radically different.

For a concrete illustration of this diversity, we will look at K. H. Miskotte's *When the Gods Are Silent* [1] and Antony Flew's *God and Philosophy*. [2] Flew is a logician, and he organizes his material accordingly. He deals with concepts, theories, arguments of all sorts, the assessments of evidence, the analyses of stances taken. Only in passing does he refer concretely to the great mass of biblical materials which parallel so many of his topics.

Miskotte is more poet than theologian, and some of his passages have an unrelievable obscurity about them. But Miskotte has in a remarkable way caught the vision of the God of Scripture, and some scholars think that this is one of the great books of our century. It is filled with insights, perspectives, angles, and interpretations that come from years and years of living with the Old Testament. Flew's God and Flew's religion are skin, bone, and dust; Miskotte's book has heart and soul and is God-filled. If the real issue is truth, as Flew pounds away, then certainly Miskotte's God is a far truer God than Flew's. Flew's typical British empiricism and resort to supposedly hard-headed logic gives the appearance of one who knows truth when he sees it and sternly resists any emotional fogging of his intellectual glasses. But this is just one theory of truth among others. Miskotte, on the other hand, seems too mystical, too poetic, too imaginative, too unchecked by logic and fact. Yet a sense of the true and living God shines powerfully through Miskotte's work that does not in Flew's.

In Holy Scripture God comes to man in a medium or a modality or a sign. The prophet or apostle may be in a special state of spiritual sensitivity such as prayer, contemplation, confession, worship, or adoration. The medium or sign may be some natural object, some natural phenomenon, some unusual phenomenon, or a miracle or a wonder. The function of revelation at this point is extremely variable. But for the most part, the event of revelation is imbedded in a history of events of revelation so that it is part of a larger context.

In this medium and in this event (event signifying more than me-

---

1. New York: Harper & Row, 1967.
2. London: Hutchinson, 1966.

dium), the revelation of God or the Word of God comes to man. It enters his cosmos by God's initiative and by God's grace. It truly comes, that is, it does make a difference. The world would be different if it had not come, and the world is different because it has come.

However, the divine action is not exhausted in God's self-revelation through dream, vision, miracle, or historical event. God the Holy Spirit is working an inner work in the prophet and apostle. It is this inner working that enables the recipient of the revelation to realize that it is a revelation, that it is God's Word to him, that this or that sign has such and such a particular meaning. In other words, the event and act of revelation in which God becomes real and in which God becomes known has an outer and an inner side. It is not only God in the burning bush but the Spirit of God in the heart of Moses.

These media and their corresponding events now belong to the past and cannot be part of man's contemporary experience. But the inspired record and authoritative witness to them is to be found in Holy Scripture. The reality of the events of revelation in the past have a quality of *re-presentation* to them. This is comparable to the testimony of a witness in a court of law. The witness gives the judge, jury, and lawyers a representative and, hence, vicarious experience of the original events. Man's encounter with the reality of the living God is now based upon the scriptural record of events revealed to him by the Holy Spirit.

We can say epigrammatically that the proof of the existence of God is Holy Scripture *if* we know what we are saying. This statement presumes an understanding of Scripture as the vicarious representative of historical events of God's action and God's Word. Through the use of such events and words the Spirit of God makes God the Reality that he is to us.

Section 15: The Mode of Reception of Divine Revelation

By this time it should be clear that the approach to the reality of God from the standpoint of Scripture is complex. It has the form of a pattern or a program and not the form of a logical proof. The reality of God involves the whole structure of the concept of revelation and redemption and has no significant meaning outside this context.

In order to understand how God's reality is known and how the knowledge of God becomes an empirical reality, revelation and salvation must be related objectively. Revelation and salvation are objective in the sense that they existed before a given man's existence and will continue after man's existence. Furthermore God's revelation and salvation not only exist prior to man's encounter, but revelation and salvation shape man's experience. Man's experience is not more fundamental than the truth of God in salvation and revelation.

Historically speaking this viewpoint is in reaction to the course of liberal theology from Schleiermacher on. During the Reformation Catholic theologians and Reformers agreed in their understanding of faith and the object of faith. Truth shapes experience; experience does not shape truth. The theology of faith and its object sets forth the norm, the pattern, the standard of experience. Not all Christian experiences are identical; every conversion to Christ is unique. But at the time of the Reformation all experiences were understood to be within the bounds set by Holy Scripture and Christian theology.

The liberal tradition reversed this. Fosdick described the Christian faith as essentially personal experiences of abiding categories. Dogmatics or theology was a reflection upon the experience, but it was of the second order and not the first.

Modern existentialist theologians follow the same pattern, but in some cases (for example, Ebeling) they have tried to preserve in some manner the abiding priority of the conceptual or theological side of Christianity. However, in general, writers of this school make faith (as existentially understood) the primary datum of Christianity and consider theology as the reflection of this faith or the contour one draws around the faith. In essence the liberal existentialist theologian maintains that while faith as the fundamental of the Christian religion remains the same, through the centuries the various theological formulations are culturally conditioned and imbued with philosophies, thought forms, and categories of the historical period. Therefore, they need to be continuously reexamined and restated for each emerging culture.

It seems to me that this approach denies the real transhistorical, transcultural Word of God or divine revelation. God's Word, God's truth, God's revelation, God's authority is immensely watered down by virtue of concepts such as "historical relativity," "the ever-shifting patterns of cultures," and "the new perspectives of later generations inspired by better views of the cosmos."

However, if the conceptual side of religion keeps changing as culture changes in its moods, interpretations, and categories, then the so-called experience of faith undergoes the same kind of historical erosion. The idea that one can admit the endless shifting of culture and its effective rendering of historical versions of Christian theology as obsolete and yet preserve some version of faith or Christian experience as always and ever valid is sheer delusion. The latter shifts around as much as the former. This is not to be blind to cultural shifts, to changes of categories, to the understanding that theological items alive to one generation can be dead to another. It is interesting to see how philosophers readily (even automatically) adjust to the cultural period of the writer (such as to some of the senseless analogies of Plato) and yet get to the heart of the philosopher's ideas. And those ideas are held as viable options today. Yet theologians seem to fall all over themselves in pointing out the cultural factors in Holy Scripture (or any given period in which a theologian writes) as if almost all is vitiated by its cultural conditioning. More than one scholar of the classics has said that if he treated the Latin and Greek classics the way theologians treat Scripture it would be the end of the classics. Nevertheless, theologians, especially since Schleiermacher, are so prone to erode the theology of Scripture and the theology of a given epic on the grounds of historical relativity.

Those theologians who believe in the abiding, unchanging internal aspects of Christian experience, as over against Christianity's culturally conditioned theology, are mistaken. These internal, abiding aspects change too. The current so-called youth rebellion or generation gap is eloquent testimony that internal attitudes can be just as historically relative and unstable as the conceptual elements of theology. The effort of the older liberals and the newer existentialists who make such a distinction are both caught in the same trap. Existential faith can shift and change around as much as Greek substance philosophy and theology.

But we must return to the main theme of this section. There is a biblical doctrine of the reception of revelation as well as a doctrine of the origin of revelation.

Generally this response is called faith, but other terms are used with it such as trust, hope, obedience, commitment, repentance, and decision. All of these terms are part of the cluster pattern of the act of receiving revelation as revelation.

Faith is assent (*assensus*) in that faith is presumed to be in something that is true. Too many modern theologians rule assent out of the experience of faith as if it represented a purely rational or intellectual or theological response. But if there is no sense of truth, no sense of meeting reality in its conceptual form, no sense of encountering God's Word which ineluctably carries the idea of truth, then the religious experience is worthless. The Book of Psalms expresses in a hundred different ways (as in Ps. 119) the refrain that the Word of God is a true Word. If there is no element of the truth in the experience of the gospel or if the existential encounter is completely existential and void of true conceptual elements, then the experience of the gospel or the kerygma is undermined and its seriousness as an experience is lost. Faith at this level means that the believer in divine revelation believes it to be true, and in believing the truth he is also encountering the living God who comes to man in truth as well as in salvation.

Faith is also decision. The decision is the response of faith in which the sinner makes a verdict, namely, that his former life was out of step with the intentions of God but from now on he will conduct his life as God would have him conduct it. This means that he decides for Christ, for the Christian ethic, and for the Christian set of values. He is willing to serve God in any way in which God would command him. He is willing to be a Christian in the total range of his life.

Faith is repentance. Repentance has been called the moral seriousness of the gospel. In the Old Testament the Hebrew word used for repentance means turning; in the New Testament repentance means rethinking, rejudging, reevaluating. But whatever the basic imagery, the concept is the same, namely, that unbelief also involves the wrong kind of moral standards and actions. Faith entails getting one's moral perspectives corrected and turned in the right direction.

Faith is also trust. However, this is not trust in a law or a custom but in a person, the person of Christ. The Reformers insisted that in addition to faith as assent there must be faith as trust in Christ. In this sense faith is personal, or faith is encounter, or faith is the authentic decision. Much is made today of faith as an I-Thou relationship following the thought of Martin Buber. If this is just a synonym for the necessary personal dimension in faith, then there is nothing wrong with the expression as each generation seeks out its own expression of this dimension of faith. But if the I-Thou relationship is taken as a serious, valid theological concept, then a protest must be registered. There are some serious problems of theory of knowledge in Buber's thought. It is unbelievable how uncritically Buber is quoted and how uncritical contemporary theology has been of Buber's theory of knowledge until recently when some theologians began criticizing him from the stance of the newer analytic theology.

The point is that faith is polydimensional in character: the believer comes to know the reality of God, he comes to know God as the living God, he comes into an authentic knowledge of God. When the biblical idea of faith in the living God (with assent, trust, hope, decision, obedience) is contrasted with belief in God's existence by virtue of the theistic proofs, such belief appears pale and spiritless.

Faith is intuition. In this context faith means directness, immediacy, direct confrontation. It is in contrast to knowledge gained by logical action, reasoning process, or experiment. In its primitive sense intuition means to look directly at something. There is no mediation between the viewer and the thing seen; or there are no logical steps from the perception of the mind to the truth of the perceived. Thus the words in Scripture that speak of man's knowing of God are words of intuition, directness, and knowing in the sense of participation. In the Old Testament the verb *know*, for example, is a euphemism for sexual intercourse. It carries a sense of immediacy and confrontation in contrast to rational deduction, inference, or theoretical or philosophical analysis.

The artist, the poet, the seer, and the novelist are closer to the biblical idea of faith than the logician, the scientist, or the philosopher. This corresponds to the nature of God and his revelation. He establishes his reality, his power, his salvation. He does not establish his existence as the *deus nudus*—"the naked God." The biblical idea of God the living God is the right one, not the philosophical notion of "the naked God."

Section 16: The Special Case of the Old Testament

In the ancient world virtually everybody believed in gods or spirits or a pantheon of gods. There is some slight evidence of atheism in the Old Testament, but not much. "The fool says in his heart, 'There is no God' " (Ps. 14:1, RSV). "They have disowned [or, belied] Yahweh" (Jer. 5:12, JB). More to the point was the practical atheism that prevailed in Israel. Men formally acknowledged that Yahweh existed but that he was indifferent to human affairs. Therefore men could sin with impunity and not be judged by Yahweh. Much of what the prophets had to say was not about the existence of Yahweh but against the practical atheism of the Israelites.

The real issue in the Old Testament was which of all the competing gods was the living Lord. The word *living* was used to indicate that God does make a difference. A god who is not living can make no difference; but a living God does make a difference. For this reason, the logically ordered proof for God's existence doesn't exist in the Old Testament.

The prophets set up certain differentia which would enable a person in doubt or confusion to determine which among the gods was the living God. The God who complied with such differentia was the living God, and the god or gods who couldn't were not gods at all. Therefore the emphasis is on the living God, for the living God can make a difference; a dead god cannot. For this reason the emphasis in the Old Testament is not on the true God (although the expression does exist in Jer. 10:10, but even here in connection with the living God) but on the living God. The living God makes a difference. So many recent discussions by philosophers or theologians in the analytic or linguistic tradition are extremely unbiblical. That they are discussing a very serious problem about the kind of language we use, or the way we use language, when we speak of God is not overlooked nor depreciated. The unbiblical character of so many of these discussions is based on the premise that the reality of God can only be known through an unimpeachable logical argument. When Amos wrote, "The lion has roared; who will not fear? The Lord God has spoken; who can but prophesy?" (Amos 3:8, RSV), he was using other criteria about the reality of God than logical ones. The same is true when Jeremiah writes, "Is not my word like fire, says the Lord, and like a hammer which breaks the rock in pieces?" (Jer. 23:29, RSV).

When certain modern writers do approach the subject of how God makes a difference, these differences are not the kind the Holy Scripture uses. Biblical differences may involve some unusual kind of psychological insight or pattern, but they are also historical, real, out there. This kind of God does make a difference. The concept of the proven God is too rationalistic (in the pejorative sense), too philosophical, too abstract, too much divorced from creation and history, to measure up to the God of Israel who really makes a difference.

Some of the biblical criteria for discerning the living God are:
The living God is the Creator; the false gods are not.
"For all the gods of the peoples are idols; but the Lord made the heavens" (Ps. 96:5, RSV).

"Beaten silver is brought from Tarshish,
    and gold from Uphaz.
They are the work of the craftsman and of the hands of the goldsmith;
    their clothing is violet and purple;
    they are all the work of skilled men.
But the Lord is the true God;
    he is the living God and the everlasting King.

At his wrath the earth quakes,
and the nations cannot endure his indignation.
Thus shall you say to them: 'The gods who did not make the heavens
and the earth shall perish from the earth and from under the heavens.'
It is he who made the earth by his power,
who established the world by his wisdom,
and by his understanding stretched out the heavens.
When he utters his voice there is a tumult of waters in the heavens,
and he makes the mist rise from the ends of the earth.
He makes lightnings for the rain,
and he brings forth the wind from his storehouses.
Every man is stupid and without knowledge;
every goldsmith is put to shame by his idols;
for his images are false,
and there is no breath in them.
They are worthless, a work of delusion;
at the time of their punishment they shall perish.
Not like these is he who is the portion of Jacob,
for he is the one who formed all things,
and Israel is the tribe of his inheritance;
the Lord of hosts is his name" (Jer. 10:9–16, RSV).

"To whom then will you liken God,
or what likeness compare with him?
The idol! a workman casts it,
and a goldsmith overlays it with gold,
and casts for it silver chains.
He who is impoverished chooses for an offering
wood that will not rot;
he seeks out a skillful craftsman
to set up an image that will not move.
Have you not known? Have you not heard?
Has it not been told you from the beginning?
Have you not understood from the foundations of the earth?
It is he who sits above the circle of the earth,
and its inhabitants are like grasshoppers;
who stretches out the heavens like a curtain,
and spreads them like a tent to dwell in" (Isa. 40:18–22, RSV).

The living God is self-existent; the idols must be sustained.

"But you who forsake the Lord,
   who forget my holy mountain,
  who set a table for [the god] Fortune
    and fill cups of mixed wine for [the god] Destiny [that he may drink
      and so be nourished]" (Isa. 65:11, RSV).

"The children gather wood, the fathers kindle fire, and the women knead dough, to make cakes for the queen of heaven [that is, for her sustenance]; and they pour out drink offerings [for the thirst] to other gods, to provoke me to anger" (Jer. 7:18, RSV).

The living God acts sovereignly in nature and yet is not a nature god.
"And you call on the name of your god and I will call on the name of the Lord; and the God who answers by fire, he is God" (1 Kings 18:24, RSV). Here the many miracles worked through Moses, Elijah, and especially Elisha could be cited, as well as the Egyptian plagues.

"For you have not come to what may be touched [as the Israelites did and hence this passage is a reflection on God's appearances in the Exodus account], a blazing fire, and darkness, and gloom, and a tempest, and the sound of a trumpet" (Heb. 12:18–19, RSV).

Yet in all the manners and ways in which the Lord made himself manifest in Israel, he is never a weather god or a nature god but the living God of revelation and redemption in the household of Israel.

The prophets taunt the idol-worshipers of their times in ways too numerous for exposition. For example, the idol is always a fabricated object; Yahweh is the Creator. The idol cannot move himself but must be carried about; God is omnipresent. The idol cannot speak but is both deaf and mute; the God of Israel is both a God that hears and a God that speaks.

The conclusion is simple but impressive: the God of Israel is a living God because when subjected to the criteria of what a living God is like the God of Israel meets these criteria; the gods and idols do not. Therefore, the God of Israel is the living and true and, therefore, existing God.

Section 17: The Special Character of God in the New Testament

Everywhere the New Testament writers presume that they are speaking and writing of the God of Israel. The essential Marcionite heresy (from Marcion, died about A.D. 160, who declared that God of the Old Testament was different from God of the New Testament—the Demiurge of the Old Covenant of Law versus the God and Father of Jesus Christ, the God of love) has been denounced as frequently as it has reappeared in the history of theology. The author of Hebrews affirms that the God who spoke in the prophets of the Old Covenant is the identical God who spoke through his Son in the New Covenant (Heb. 1:1–2). Therefore everything that the Old Testament says about God, especially in reference to the gods, goddesses, and idols of the Greco-Roman culture of the New Testament, remains valid and in force and need not be repeated.

Furthermore, there is a great theological overlap between the Old Testament and the New Testament. (1) Although the New Testament does declare that the ceremonial and dietetic teaching of the Old Testament are not binding in the Christian church, neither the God of the Old Testament nor the essential theology of the Old Testament is repudiated. (2) The writers of the New Testament frequently cite the Old Testament directly and indirectly as the authoritative Word of God for the church. (3) The fundamentals of Old Testament faith are the crossing points for Jews coming to Christ (Heb. 6:1–4). The life of faith is the same for both Testaments (Heb. 11). The appeal of the New Testament to the fulfilled word of the Old Covenant in its own pages, its appeal to fulfilled typology, and its use of Old Testament apocalyptic images and symbols all show the continuity of theology in the two Testaments.

There are, however, three special emphases on the nature of God in the New Testament which further establish the reality of God.

In the New Testament God is known as Father. This is not the assertion or affirmation of another name for God. But it expresses both the attitude and the activity of God and therefore refers to the reality of God's action in the world. This is empirical stuff, empirical in the sense that things happen in this world by God's fatherly act that otherwise would not happen. Certainly *father* in a human sense is not just a word or title given by children to parents. To be a father is to do the things a father does. In the language of a trite old Americanism, "He brings home the bacon." So God as Father in the New Testament indicates numerous things which God does specifically, concretely, actually in this cosmos among his children, so that his great reality is beyond doubt to his children.

In the New Testament God is known incarnationally, that is, Christologically. If in the widest sense Holy Scripture is the supreme proof of the existence of God because of its sustained record of God coming into man's cosmos and making a difference, so the Incarnation of God in Christ is the most specific proof for the reality, the actuality of God.

(1) First, it is an unspeakable act of real condescension. God truly bends himself low, humiliates himself in human flesh, accommodates himself to worldly existence, subjects himself to the factors of human life. This makes a difference. This is not a religious idea or a theological abstraction. The Incarnation is an event; it is an occurrence; it is history; it has a spatial coordinate; it has a temporal coordinate; and it has a worldly authentic backdrop. This is certainly not the God of religious liberalism who, bound by the law of the uniformity of nature by the liberals, could not make a difference in the cosmos. Nor is the God of Bultmann and other existentialist theologians, who with the liberals bind the arms of God with the doctrine of the uniformity of nature, the biblical God. Modern theologians may feel more comfortable in a world of science, technology, and critical philosophy with a God who never steps out of line with the course of nature, but they have taken such a position by surrendering that kind of God who can make a difference. But such a God is the only really believable God in a world of science, technology, and critical philosophy where making a difference is a fundamental criterion for anything that claims to be a reality. The Father of the New Testament is such a believable God.

(2) It is a real entrance into the human cosmos. This is expressed by the virgin birth. The virgin birth is no speculation about the Incarnation's modality (so Brunner). It is not an attempt to show how the condescension of the Incarnation took place. Nor is it myth (so Bultmann). It is not an attempt to state in worldly terms an existential or a divine action. It is a worldly event; it is a divine action. It is concretely, specifically, eventlike the means and manner by which God does truly become incarnate. It is not a mythological witness (so Boslooper) to the reality of the Incarnation. It is not a mythological or mysterious or symbolic way of expressing the Incarnation. It is, to the contrary, the mode, the means, the channel by which God the Son does become incarnate, does enter the human world, and does come into the sphere of man. It thus makes a difference—a historical difference, an empirical difference, a cosmic difference. The attempt to maintain the Incarnation and at the same time reject a virgin birth is to risk an Incarnation that does not really make a difference. There are very few theologians who maintain the conception by the Holy Spirit without the virgin birth. Unfortunately, when the virgin birth is written off for one reason or another,

the Incarnation is seldom left untouched but it too is subjected to a radical reinterpretation which downgrades it from a real Incarnation to some form of the special manifestation of God in human life.

(3) The Incarnation is the presupposition of the public ministry of Jesus Christ. Here again the Incarnation made a difference. The words, speeches, remarks, parables, prophetic utterances, and wisdom sayings of Jesus Christ are revelation. As revelation they make a difference. This is not a case of the Absentee Gardener but the public ministry of God Incarnate. The sayings are not original in the sense that Jesus first said them. Many of them are found in the Old Testament or in rabbinical literature. Their uniqueness is that they receive Christ's imprimatur of truth. They are lifted from the realm of religious maxim to the plane of revelation. They are given a new authority, the authority of the Son of God.

Beside the words of Jesus Christ are the revelatory actions of Christ. In his various actions he revealed God's attitude of love or grace or displeasure or wrath. The quality of the life of Christ incorporates the qualities of the last Adam and therefore the norm of all human qualities that please God. But more than that, Jesus' miracles, wonders, and signs showed that what he taught in word was a teaching with a reality. So much of the discussion of the miracles of Christ lose the whole point of them. Such discussions deal with historical ambiguities of reliable reporting (so Hume), or with man's mythological projection outward of his inner existential experience (so Bultmann), or a commentary on the unrestrained mytho-poetic fantasy of the apostles or church writers who composed the Gospels.

The miracles and signs of Christ made a difference. They showed that this man spoke with the authority of God; they blazed forth for all to see that this man's word was a word of reality; they indicated that what this man claimed in speech was also true for all men and before God. They showed that this man's promises were not nice words or poetic words but words of reality, changing the course of historical possibilities and marking out the actions, deeds, and doings of God in our world.

So many articles on miracles or books on miracles miss this point completely. They are written so unrealistically, so academically, so divorced from the historical situation, so concerned with philosophical sophistries. How does Christ communicate with an uneducated public? How are the chains of sin—moral or intellectual—broken? How can Christ make his words the imperial words of God to them? Can love be understood only as pure verbal declaration with no powerful manifestation of that love? What kind of evidence counts with a man of that culture and that historical period? What is wrong with the mentality of a man who wants the witness of the truth of God in the first century in such a sophisticated form that only a twentieth-century man could grasp it? Again, what blind spot is in the scholar who sets up his standards of what he will believe and not believe and imposes them on a culture two thousand years before he was born?

(4) The Incarnation lead through the public ministry to the cross, *and the cross certainly made a difference before God, and before man, and in Christ.* The cross had this unique character. Outwardly, humanly, and historically it was but another crucifixion. Death by some sort of impalement on wooden stakes has a long history, so crucifixion was not new to the Jews (Phoenicians, Persians, Egyptians, Carthaginians, Indians, Assyrians, Greeks, Germans, or Romans). On one occasion two thousand were crucified; on another occasion, thirty-six hundred. At the time of the capture of Jerusalem by Titus, the Roman soldiers not only ran out of wood to make crosses on which to hang the Jews, they also ran out of places to bury the crosses in the ground.

As a mode of execution the crucifixion of Christ was then completely ordinary. Yet from the biblical standpoint it was the redemption of the world, the most unique event in the history of the human race. This redemption was not accomplished because of the unusual nature of Christ's death; nor did his great physical sufferings secure man's redemption. Other people have suffered more in terms of sheer pain, and the duration of the pain has been more extended. But Christ's death was before God. It was a sacrifice for the sins of the world; it was an atonement, an act of reconciliation. It therefore has made a difference in human history. It made a difference before God who sorrowed over his creation and loved it. It made a difference in Christ, for now having suffered he has become the Savior of the world. It made a difference for the world, for from out of these sufferings came the gospel and from the gospel came the church which became the visible manifestation of the change the cross made in the world.

(5) *The Incarnation comes to its clearest revelation in the resurrection, ascension, and session* (Christ seated at the right hand of God the Father). Certainly there is a difference here in creation and redemption. Regardless of the efforts of critics of all sorts to destroy the evidence for the risen Christ, in 1 Corinthians 15:5–8 the record stands sure. This passage is not an interpolation of the church or the interpretation of the church or the creation of a non-Pauline hand. It is the list of the Jerusa-

lem church of what that church deemed to be the solid historical basis for faith in the bodily risen Christ. J. G. Davies's work, *He Ascended into Heaven*, shows the immense amount of New Testament materials that directly affirm the ascension or indirectly affirm it in that what is said presupposes it. The ascension does not rest on a few verses in Luke and Acts.

The importance of these matters of Christology for the knowledge of God and his reality is exceedingly great. Christ is the Logos who comes from the bosom of the Father and declares his counsel which must therefore include the reality of God. In John 1:1, Christ is declared the Logos, the visible, hearable speech of God himself, the Supreme Revealer of the reality of God. John 1:14 asserts that the divine Logos of John 1:1 is nonetheless God-incarnate appearing as Jesus of Nazareth. In his public ministry, Jesus makes the reality of God incontrovertible (compare John 1:18).

Here again the biblical approach to God, namely the reality of the living God, is seen in marked contrast to the philosophical approach of proving the existence of God. The biblical approach indicates that it is God's initiative which seeks man; it is God's condescension and humiliation which stretches out toward man. God comes into man's own orbit and discloses life, salvation, prayer, and community. One of Kierkegaard's complaints is that he intended his writings to promote genuine faith in Christ and not become the basis for other articles, books, debates, and academic discussions. The same could be said of the Christian faith. It has its intellectual or conceptual or rational side. But to treat its themes only academically, only as problems in scholarship, or only as topics for theses or dissertations or books is to betray its very essence, to wound it at its very heart.

The knowledge of God in Holy Scripture is Trinitarian. Unfortunately this doctrine has suffered from gross misinterpretation. Naïve utterances from the pulpit on the subject amount to an affirmation of tri-theism. The doctrine of the Trinity has been justified by analogies that in no way actually support the doctrine. On the other hand theologians influenced by Hatch (1835–89) and by Harnack, who picked up this part of Hatch's thesis, affirm that the doctrine of the Trinity is a Greek formulation using Greek philosophical terms and Greek substance philosophy.

No theologian denies that numerous problems exist concerning the doctrine of the Trinity. *Persona* is an old Latin term; what is its present counterpart? The use of the word *modus* with reference to the Trinity leads to modalism. What modern term says what *modus* intends to say without becoming modalistic? What is the modern term for *substantia?* What do such expressions as *eternal generation* or *eternal procession* mean, and what modern English words may we use?

Modern efforts to preserve the Trinity by saying that it speaks of the complexity of the idea of God or the richness of the idea of God are betrayals of the Trinity. True, the Trinity suggests the richness and the complexity of the idea of God, but that is only a preliminary observation. Theologians who restrict their idea of the Trinity to God's richness of activity do not do justice to the Trinity.

The Trinity is to be understood in the manner in which it expresses the character of God's revelation and redemption. This is its natural habitat. It speaks of the unity of God in the triunity of his action (the so-called economic Trinity). But this economic Trinity makes sense only as it is the manifestation of the real (ontological) Trinity. It is one God who is Speaker, the Word spoken, and the Word assimilated just as it is one God who is the Redeemer, the Savior, and the Realizer of salvation. Yet these are not just functions, modes, activities, but in the mystery of the early language of the creeds they are Persons. The Father does not die on the cross; the Son is not the electing God; and the Spirit is not our Father to whom we pray. It is the one God in revelation and salvation—the meaning of the divine *perichoresis,* the "penetration" of the persons of the Trinity into each other, the *circumincessio.* It is the divine Trinity in their unsharable acts in revelation and redemption.

This is not theological gobbledegook but a profound doctrine of the reality of God, of the participation of God in our cosmos, of the inbreaking of God into our consciousness, of the creating of God in man not only a sense of his existence but of his reality, of his salvation, of his indwelling, of his providence, of his response to human prayer. For this reason the real believer considers philosophical ventures into the existence of God to be rather arid. The living God makes a difference; he reveals; he saves; he creates communion; he enters into dialogue with man through Holy Scripture.

Hence, the richness of the doctrine of the Trinity is not mere theology, or mere historical theology, or mere word-juggling, but part of the marvelous way in which the living God of Holy Scripture becomes present to the experience and consciousness of man. The Trinitarian God becomes a living Reality to the real believer.

VIII
The Problem of Evil
and the Christian Faith

Section 18: Theological and Philosophical Solutions

It could be said that in the history of the philosophy of religion the supreme achievement was a proof for the existence of God. Around this issue has grown a large literature both in defense and in refutation of the proof or proofs.

This problem has not disappeared, but another one has appeared to compete with it, namely, the problem of evil. The problem of evil has always been with theology and philosophy, but it has taken on a new dimension. It has been recently claimed that the existence of evil positively disproves the existence of God. Heretofore the existence of God was refuted on the logical imperfections in the arguments. Now it is claimed that there is logical proof that God does not exist. The claim is that the existence of God and the existence of evil are contradictory.

The argument against the existence of a good and loving God is primarily as follows:

(1) Theistic faith asserts that God is good (that is, he does not will evil) ; that God is wise (he wouldn't create a universe that was a botch of things) ; and that God is powerful (he wouldn't let anything exist that is beyond his power).

(2) Yet evils of all sorts exist that no good God would permit, that no wise God would include in his plans, and that no powerful God would allow to exist.

(3) Therefore, since it is contradictory to assert a good, wise, and

powerful God in the face of irrational, uncontrolled evil, the God of traditional theism does not exist—Christian, Muslim, or Jewish.

The argument against the existence of a good, wise, and powerful God is made more impressive by indicating certain kinds of suffering that are void of any redemptive, ethical, or moral purpose. (1) Babies, children, and animals may suffer terrible pain, but because they have no real mind, there is no spiritual good that can come from their suffering. (2) Suffering in an adult over a limited period of time may increase his spirituality, but when the suffering is prolonged indefinitely, no more spiritual growth takes place. (3) Degenerative diseases of the brain or nervous system destroy the sufferer's mind so that he is unable to gain good from suffering. (4) The pain a person has may be so intense that the person is too numbed to do any kind of thinking or meditating that would increase his spirituality. (5) Two or more diseases may strike the same person, and if to treat one is to excite the other, the person is likely to become too confused to do any kind of thinking that would be of spiritual profit.

In such cases the pain and suffering is so great that no spiritual or moral or religious growth is possible. Therefore any explanation of evil at this point is self-refuting because the very nature of the case prevents spiritual growth. It is therefore maintained that in situations like these it cannot be said that God is good, for there is terrible evil which he could prevent and doesn't; and the possibility of the sufferer to gain in spirituality is impossible because he is in no condition to do the thinking or reflecting that would increase his spirituality.

Theodicy as a topic is as old as religion and theology. As a particular term it stems from Leibniz. Pierre Bayle (1647–1706) led a very hectic personal and academic career reflecting much of the philosophical and theological chaos of the times. His most famous work was his *Dictionnaire Historique et Critique* (1695, 1697). A major part of this work was a discussion of the problem of evil. Many took it upon themselves to reply to Bayle, but the most important to do so was Leibniz. He responded by writing his *Theodicy* in 1710 in which he invented the word *theodicy*. It is composed of two Greek words, *theos* (God) and *dikē* (justice) and means the justification or the exoneration of the ways of God with men, particularly as they center in the problem of evil (*An Essay on Theodicy about the goodness of God, the freedom of man, and the origin of evil*, 1710).

Right or wrong, Leibniz's essay has become a definitive work on the problem of evil, and most serious discussions of the problem of evil deal in some part with Leibniz's solution. The essential purpose of all theodicies is to show that regardless of the sufferings, tragedies, mysteries, evils, enigmas, puzzles, and catastrophes that beset the universe, and particularly man, God's rule is nevertheless holy, wise, good, and just. Philosophically this is termed *the problem of evil*.

A word about the relationship of sin and evil must be mentioned. Evil is the destruction of the good. A worker whose arm is severed from his body by some piece of power equipment in a factory has suffered an evil. A person who performs an act contrary to some moral code has sinned. All sin is evil because all sin is some form of destruction of good within a person. To lie is not just to misrepresent the facts, but lying does something to the fiber of the self, be it ever so small. However, not all evil is sin. A rope or cable that frays and gives way may result in the death of a man. Although this is evil, it is not sin. The problem of sin is included in the problem of evil, but the problem of evil is more comprehensible than the problem of sin. This is why the serious discussions concern evil rather than sin although sin too is a very aggravated problem for theistic belief.

This exposition will be concerned with the problem of evil as it relates to Christian faith. It is not possible to make a complete separation of the philosophical problem of evil and the Christian discussion of evil, but some sort of selection will be attempted.

Section 19: Evil As Metaphysical Lack

If God is good, wise, and powerful, how is it possible for evil to exist in his creation? If a bacteriologist has all possible chemicals at his disposal, how can one germ survive after he has purified an operating room? If the perfect maid were to clean a house, how could one speck of offending dust remain? If a chemist could coat all the parts of a machine with a perfect alloy, how could one speck of rust appear on any part of the mechanism?

God is greater than any bacteriologist or maid or chemist, yet evil does mar his creation. What is the ultimate answer to this question?

The traditional Christian answer is that only God is God. This means that only God has perfect being; only God has plenitude or fullness of being; God and God alone is the highest being. This lack of being, this partiality of being, this less-than-God being possesses some kind of a lack, some kind of a vacuum, some indefinable deficiency, some shortcoming of being which is the metaphysical possibility of sin. This is what Leibniz called metaphysical evil for only God has the plenitude of being.

To phrase it another way, only God is full being, perfect being, and absolute being. Therefore he is eternally fixed in goodness, sinlessness, justice, honor, and glory.

"In him is no darkness at all" (1 John 1:5). *Darkness* here means that nothing evil or demonic or earthly, which are the possibilities of evil, are in God.

At this point philosophers and theologians start to stutter. They believe in the reality of a good God, and they recognize evil as evil and nothing less than evil. But what is that possible impossibility, that non-God in God's universe, that in some way makes the space and the situation for evil to come into being? How can the void be the area in which evil may come and at the same time somehow not be that evil? How can the vacuum of being be that vacuum that gives evil its leverage and somehow not be the catalyst of evil? The rays of the sun weaken and spread as they speed away from the sun, and into this darkness evil may come, and yet how can the vacancy of darkness generate evil?

This is rooted in Neoplatonic thought. Neoplatonism is a pantheistic version of the philosophy of Plato developed in Rome during the Christian era. Its leading scholar was Plotinus (205–70, author of the *Enneads* or "nines" after the literary structure of his philosophy). Plotinus had an enormous influence on Augustine who was the greatest influence on theological thought of the Middle Ages outside the Scriptures. Plotinus also influenced Dionysius, supposedly the convert of Paul (Acts 17:34). It is now known that Dionysius was a sixth-century writer but his works (*The Celesterial Hierarchy, The Ecclesiastical Hierarchy, The Divine Names, The Mystical Theology*) were taken as genuine for centuries including Thomas Aquinas. Much Neoplatonic thought got into Christian theology through these writings too.

Section 20: Evil As Instrumental

Among Christians the most popular theory of evil is that in the wisdom and providence of God, God makes evil contribute to the total good of the universe. Such a theory is called an instrumental theory because it maintains that God uses evil as an instrument for human good even though just how this is done may remain inscrutable to man. This theory may be illustrated from different perspectives. Appeal is made to the following verses: "You meant evil against me; but God meant it for good" (Gen. 50:20, RSV); "We know that in everything God works for good" (Rom. 8:28, RSV).

Aesthetic version. When evil is considered by itself, it appears irrational and contrary to the goodness of God. But if seen in a total perspective, it contributes to the beauty of the universe. It is instrumental then to the total vision of the beauty of the cosmos.

A bowl of pepper would be a very distressing meal. But a sprinkling of pepper on a steak adds greatly to the flavor of the steak. Listening to somebody practice his percussion instruments can create maximum irritation, but in a concert the sound of the drum or the clash of cymbals adds just that dramatic touch to make the piece even more beautiful. The typical brown background of the older Dutch artists is ugly in itself, but it contributes immeasurably to the beauty of the face extracted from it. The black velvet upon which jewels are placed makes the jewels sparkle ever so much better.

Still another example of the aesthetic theory (that is, what is ugly or evil in part really adds to the beauty of the whole) is the analogy taken from rug making. The threads on the bottom side of a rug crisscross in a haphazard manner from which no design can be deciphered. The top side reveals a beautiful pattern taking shape. Man sees only the bottom side of the rug with its patternless maze of threads, but God sees the top side with its design. So man trusts that the crisscross of threads he sees on the bottom side are really forming an intricate pattern on the top side which he cannot see.

There are problems in connection with the aesthetic approach to the problem of evil. It is put together in such a way that no possible objection can be made. Since man can see only the bottom side of the rug, he can always assume that from the top side a pattern is being woven. But as long as the top side is never seen on this earth, no real check can be made. Essentially this approach illustrates a thesis, but it does not present a solution. In logic illustrations are not proofs even though they may be of high educational worth.

Dualistic version. Any instrumental theory of evil means that as irrational as evil may seem to be it nevertheless produces good. In the attempt to show how evil does eventually produce good, different kinds of solutions have been offered. Dualism is another version of the effort to show how evil eventually produces good.

There have been philosophical dualisms, religious dualisms, and Christian dualisms. Zoroastrianism was a dualism prominent in Iran five hundred years before Christ. Manicheism was a dualism of the Western world dating from the third Christian century. In his youth Augustine believed in Manicheism.

Dualism as a theory of evil means that there is a conflict in the universe and in human history. Light struggles with darkness; good struggles with evil; God struggles with the devil and/or demons; truth struggles with error; sin struggles with righteousness; spirit struggles with flesh. Man lives his life in this conflict and therefore suffers from evils. Inherent in dualism is the presupposition that eventually good will conquer evil, and in this conquest a great good will emerge that could never have existed if there had not been a conflict.

If dualism is a conflict built into the universe itself, it is called a metaphysical dualism. If dualism is not built into the universe but exists only in a limited time with a limited force, it is called a relative or instrumental dualism.

There is an apparent, a relative, a partial, a limited, an instrumental dualism reflected in Scripture (but not a metaphysical dualism)—God and the devil, good angels and fallen angels, higher powers or spirits of goodness and demons or devils, righteousness and sin, Holy Spirit and sinful flesh, and saints and sinners. This dualism is described as relative because there is no question who is the winner in the conflict: the omnipotent God is. Such is the clear and final message of the Book of Revelation.

The problem at this point is to decide if this relative dualism is also an instrumental dualism by means of which the good of the universe is made apparent, and man by struggling with evil is able to achieve a good he never could if evil never existed. Accordingly this relative, instrumental dualism is capable of being expressed different ways.

Definition theory. Man would never know good if he did not know evil. A man created in goodness, eternally protected from evil, would have no appreciation of goodness. Therefore evil is introduced into the universe so that man may experience evil and in so doing come to know good. He is therefore eternally better for having experienced evil, for he now knows the real character of the good.

Perhaps this is the meaning of Augustine's "O blessed guilt!" Only the person who has known pain knows the blessedness of morphine. Centuries ago morphine was called the gift of God because it was the. only known substance that could arrest the most terrible of human pains. And so only those who have known evil, shame, depravity, sin, and guilt really understand love, redemption, forgiveness, pardon, and salvation.

Sinless, holy, perfect creatures fixed into an eternal goodness would then be essentially superficial, if not even boring, creatures. Only Augustines and Luthers and Pascals and Kierkegaards are the authentic saints, the real persons.

Struggle theory. Character comes only in contest. Hence the world is filled with snakes and beasts that man may learn courage. There are storms and blights so that man may learn resourcefulness. There are temptations so that man may develop courage. There is evil, sin, and injustice so that man may develop character and love for fellow-man.

Calvin's theory. Calvin's theory is one which has to be decoded from his writings. Very important in understanding Calvin at this point are his two essays on predestination and providence published by Cole as *Calvin's Calvinism.* There is also a treatment of Calvin's theory in Hick's *Evil and the God of Love.*

All that is done in this world is done for the glory of God. Evil is not something that slipped unexpectedly into the universe posing an unexpected problem for God. God has decreed this whole world order to reveal and promote his glory and also his love and compassion for man. Hence, evil functions strictly instrumentally and is never out of the control of God. Evil is therefore restricted, limited, relative, and instrumental. In the total scheme of things, including the course of human history, evil does promote good.

As the foil of God, evil is instrumental in revealing God's glory, his power, his wisdom, and his love. If we come across some very baffling cases that seem utterly to defy any attempt to show that they can promote good, Calvin takes refuge in the secret counsels of God. If we knew those counsels, the situation would cease to baffle us. Therefore, we must retain our faith in God's love and sovereignty in even the blackest of nights.

Hick thinks that although Calvin might have a comforting word for the elect he fails to have a word of comfort or concern or love for the entire world. Niesel (*The Theology of Calvin*) and Wendel (*Calvin: The Origins and Development of his Religious Thought*) insist that Calvin included the non-Christian in his theodicy. Perhaps it can be said that in systematic theology Calvin makes a good case, but in pastoral theology his theodicy is not one that would readily give people peace of mind. Secret counsels have little comforting power.

Leibniz's theory. Leibniz was a man of many remarkable achievements. He has been called the last of the polymaths. A polymath was a person who knew all there was to know, the scholars' scholar. But knowledge has increased so much since Leibniz's day that it is no longer possible for a man to be a polymath. Among Leibniz's achievements was an expertise in mathematics, especially calculus. In calculus the mathematician is dealing with infinitesimal specks of space, with the concept of continuity, and with the concept of infinity. Leibniz attempted to solve a number of his philosophical problems by using the concepts of calculus as his model.

Suppose we think of God as the Supreme Mathematician. Before he creates the world he goes into his think tank and determines what his basic rules will be in creating the world. Being a God of love, his first concern is that creation express the maximum good. But good is something that emerges out of a context of things or it is the product of a situation. At this point God began to think as the Supreme Mathematician, guided by the concepts of calculus. Being God he can think of an infinity of worlds strung out like a string of pearls with each world differing from the one before it and after it in an infinitely small way. Each of these worlds will possess a measure of good. Out of an infinity of possible worlds, God picks out that one combination that contains the greatest amount of good. Any variation to the right or left of this world would lower the amount of good and would not be the best possible world.

This was no abstract or arbitrary decision of God. A world is a complex of many things and good exists within this complex. God chose that complex of things which would produce the greatest amount of good. This brings us to the concept of compossibility. Compossibility is concerned with how a number of factors can exist together harmoniously so as to produce good or how factors must be balanced off against each other to get the best possible combination.

Every manufacturer of an automobile must face the problem of compossibility. A big engine will give the car power, but it will also cost more to operate. A small engine will be cheap to operate but will not give that burst of power necessary in a crisis situation on the highway. If the car has a long wheelbase, it will ride smoothly, but then it will be harder to park. But if the car is too short, it will bounce too much. If it has luxury interiors, they will last a long time, but it will raise the price of the car. If poor materials are used, the price of the car is reduced, but then the customers will start complaining of rips and tears and worn spots. So every car is a product of compossibility. Something must be given up at one point to gain advantage at another point. The best possible car is the car which vectors out the best possible way all the factors involved in compossibility.

God chose this present universe because it yields the most good. But it yields the most good in terms of compossibility. It is the best possible compossible world! God could eliminate cancer. But this would lower the good in the world for God thought of every possible world including the exact one in which we live but without cancer. The elimination of cancer lowered the good so many millimeters. Eliminate any evil you can think of. God has already thought of that universe and saw that the elimination of that evil lowered the good in the universe. So this is not the best world abstractly conceived. It is the best compossible world in which the vectoring out of the factors of a world produce the greatest amount of good.

Leibniz meant the most good cosmically. A person may suffer a great evil in which he experiences pain and agony. Leibniz, however, is thinking of the level of cosmic good or the quantity of cosmic good so that no one person is able to see that *his* life is the best possible life. In Leibniz's system, metaphysical lack is thus cosmic lack and the possibility that evil or sin may exist. When men as a matter of fact do sin, then metaphysical evil has become moral evil. And from moral evil comes natural evil such as tragedies, earthquakes, and death.

There is yet another facet to Leibniz's thought. One of the problems that Plato raised was how a thought in the mind of one man was transmitted to the mind of another man so that both men had the same thought. This is one of the perpetual problems of philosophy, and it has not been solved in our century. It is more ignored than resolved. Leibniz did not think that one thought could be transmitted from one man to another man by any sort of chain of communication. Each person was in his own cell, his own cubicle. And this cell (which he called a *monad*) had no windows out of which it could peer nor wires connected to other minds. God caused all these monads to experience the same universe and thus have common experiences. This is known as the theory of preestablished harmony. Even though each person is a windowless monad, we all experience the same universe because God has preharmonized the interior experiences of all these monads. This is the basis of community and fellowship and co-humanity. But it also means that God has preharmonized all things for good. So this a second way in which it can be argued that in spite of appearances God's rule of the universe is just and fair and good.

Soul-making. It has not been uncommon in the history of theology to regard Adam as a superior person. The sign of this was Adam's power to look at an animal and give it its proper species name (Gen. 2:19–20). The famous British preacher Robert South made the classic remark of this attitude toward Adam when he said, "An Aristotle was but the rubbish of an Adam, and Athens but the rudiments of Paradise" (1634–1716: *Sermons*, Vol. I, ii).

An alternate theory derives from Irenaeus (circa 130–200, Bishop of Lyons) in which Adam is seen as green, immature, roughly shaped. His destiny in life was to become the mature man, the realized human being. Therefore, life in this world was to be a life, in later terms, of soul-making. Thus the hardships and evils of life were to be the instrument through which man would become a mature soul. Souls are made only in a universe of the rough and tumble, of pain and struggle, of evil and darkness. From such is forged the man God had in mind as the goal of history.

There is no question that the concept of soul-making has been a basic concern in the entire history of the church. Life on this earth is some kind of probationary experience. Arminian theology considers soul-making a central concept. Whether it can also be a theodicy is another question.

The theology of religious liberalism is very sympathetic with the soul-making theory. It has been accused of the upward Fall. Between the primates (popularly speaking, the monkeys) and man were a series of prehumans. The presupposition here is the theory of evolution and particularly as it applies to man. At some point in the development of man, the prehuman brain attained the power of reflection. Man could think out his problems rather than solving them by random behavior. But this power to reflect led to another power: the power to see actions as right or wrong. Morality was born!

Man fell upward. As first a beast and then as a prehuman, he had learned to solve his problems by action or reflection. But when he felt good about doing some things and bad about doing others, he crossed the threshold of pure thinking to moral thinking. Even though he felt guilty when he did the wrong thing, the very fact that he felt guilty meant that he had added a new faculty to his developing sense, namely a moral faculty. In attaining this moral faculty and learning its reality by a sense of shame or guilt in performing certain acts, man fell upward. He began the long, spiritual evolution of soul-making. The eventual product was a man equally developed in his moral judgments as he was in his rational judgments.

Some speculative biologists believe that man's physical evolution is at an end, and now evolution becomes man's moral evolution (that is, soul-making). However, some biologists say that man's body and brain will evolve to yet a higher level. If he does, he not only increases his rational powers but he increases his moral and spiritual powers. Soul-making at one point in history then gives way to higher and perhaps very different ways of soul-making.

Section 21: The Reality of Freedom and Evil

One of the most illuminating discussions of the problem of evil, historically, philosophically, and theologically is to be found in A. M. Fairbairn's *A Philosophy of the Christian Religion.*[1] What is stated in the succeeding paragraphs is following through with a suggestion by Fairbairn.

Holy Scripture states that man is in the image of God. This must not be taken to be a nice compliment about man or an exalted statement of man's nature. It means that whatever man possesses as the divine image he possesses freedom. If he does not possess freedom, he is not in the image of God whatever else nice things one may want to say of the concept of man being in the image of God.

Freedom, to be real freedom, must be freedom to opposites. A restricted or hedged-in or confined freedom may well exist, as perhaps with an animal, but this cannot be true of man in the image of God. Freedom must be freedom to radical opposites, that is, to sin or to holiness, to good or to evil, to the devil or to God. If one puts shackles on man's freedom, he has destroyed any real sense of man being in the image of God. Therefore evil must be a real possibility for man, for only in this radical possibility is he really free; and only as he is really free is he in the image of God.

Some recent philosophers of religion have said that it is not contradictory to create a man who could not sin, nor is it contradictory to create a world in which there is no evil. As logical as such a universe might be, the instinctive response, right or wrong, is that it would be a boring and trivial universe. I think Fairbairn would say such thinking is academic in the poorest sense of the word and scholastic in the poorest sense of that word. Theodicy deals with the world we have. What the

---

1. New York: Macmillan, 1902.

Christian heart wants to hear, and what the questioning non-Christian wants to know, is what the Christian faith can say that is meaningful or helpful with the actual evil and sin in the world which, in Christian teaching, is the creation of God.

Section 22: Evil As a Given

In philosophy the *given* is what is there. Sometimes it means the facts of the case, or the data, or the sensate (things received through our sensory organs). It is something presented to us over which we have no control as far as it is something which comes to us.

Some theologians have felt that evil is a given in the universe and therefore in no need of justification or explanation. It has been given many names: nonbeing, an irrational surd, an evolutionary drag, the Nothingness, the sludge or dregs of the universe, the opacity of the universe, the shadow of creation. Perhaps the most difficult and incomprehensible part of Barth's *Church Dogmatics* is the section in which he wrestles with Nothingness.

Other theologians are more venturesome. The problem is in God himself. God has a shadow or a dark side in his Being. God himself is in the God-making process and faces shadows in his own nature. So he with man has a common battle to fight to achieve ultimate wholeness.

Some theologians try to lessen the sharp contrast between a God of infinite power and love and the existence of terrible evils by making God finite. An infinite God fighting evil appears as shadowboxing, but a finite God battling with great courage against cosmic evil is a believable God. If a theologian believes that evil is a sheer given, he does not resign himself to evil. He believes that part of his mission in life is to fight evil in all of its manifestations. So whether it is personal sin, emotional disturbance, social injustice, political corruption, or a natural catastrophe, he joins the battle to overcome and eliminate evil in its every manifestation.

Perhaps evil as a given is but an alternate version of the notion of a cosmic fall. Before human history or before the creation of a spatial-temporal universe, there was a rebellion in heaven. At that time the darkness, the irrational surd, the mysterious shadow that falls over all human history and life came into existence. Theologians of previous centuries used such chapters from Holy Scripture as Isaiah 14, Ezekiel 28, and Revelation 12 to prove that the notion of a cosmic fall was a biblical idea. N. P. Williams in his classic *The Ideas of the Fall and of Original Sin*[2] leans in this direction.

There are also many versions of the Golden Age. Life now is lived under the curse and blight of evil, but it was not always so. Originally man lived in a glorious era known by many names but generally called the Golden Age. But there was some sort of falling out, some sort of division, some unexpected intrusion, and the Golden Age came to an end. Then history, penetrated with evil as we now experience it, began.

Call it the Given, or the Cosmic Fall, or the Golden Age, but something prehistorical happened which is recorded in no authentic history book of the time of the occasion. But it happened. Evil has come into man and his history. And he has to take it as part of human history and personal life like the air he breathes and the food he eats.

Section 23: Evil As Christologically Alleviated

The first nation that embraced Christianity as its national religion was Armenia. To say that one was an Armenian and not a Christian was to speak a contradiction. In 1895 the Christian world was shocked by the terrible persecution of the Armenians by the Turks. To help all Christians to understand evil and the atrocities suffered by the Armenians, Sir Robert Anderson wrote a book called *The Silence of God*.[3] The book was so compassionately and compellingly written that it went through nine editions.

Anderson's main point was that God revealed the absolute supreme love that he has for man at the cross. Here the deepest word of grace was said; the clearest intention of God to save man revealed; the clearest revelation of the eternal love of God set forth. What more is left to be said? Nothing! Therefore God is silent because he has said the clearest thing possible at the cross of his love, goodness, grace, mercy, pity, and redemption. God's silence will be ended, but it will be ended in the final days of the revelation of his wrath. Until that day, and under the present life in the silence of God, we are not to be perplexed by atrocities and evil. God's love in Christ and his cross cannot be called in question. Therefore the Christian rests his heart about evil and atrocities and barbarities in the sure knowledge of God's love at the cross. If he can

---

2. London: Longman-Greens, 1929.
3. Grand Rapids: Kregel Publications, 1952.

trust God here in the clarity of his revelation, he can trust God at those instances in history where he cannot see with any clarity the love or goodness of God. "If God is silent now it is because Heaven has come down to earth, the climax of Divine revelation has been reached, there is no reserve of mercy yet to be unfolded. He has spoken his last word of love and grace. . . . Men point to the sad incidents of human life on earth, and they ask 'Where is the love of God?' God points to that Cross as the unreserved manifestation of love so inconceivably infinite as to answer every challenge and silence all doubt for ever."[4]

Incidents of evil call into question the love and goodness of God. The cross is not an explanation of evil, a philosophical resolve of the problem of evil, but the answer to the question. In Christ and his cross the goodness and love of God is apparent, and therefore in those terrible tragedies where God seems silent or absent, Christian man is not disturbed at his foundation even though he too may have his spasms of perplexity and doubt. The love and goodness of the cross is a greater assurance of God's love than any conceivable tragedy can be a denial of that love and goodness.

Historically speaking this is remarkable in that Karl Barth has followed a similar Christological approach to the problem of theodicy and evil.

Interpreting Barth is always very difficult because he discusses the same subject in many different places. If an interpreter of Barth reads one such section and thinks that this is all Barth has to say on the subject, he cannot help but misinterpret Barth. This is apparently what happened when Edward H. Madden and Peter H. Hare interpreted Barth in their work *Evil and the Concept of God.*[5]

Barth is against all attempts of natural reason or philosophy or philosophy of religion to interpret those great theological concepts that can really be known by divine revelation through its witness in Holy Scripture. Philosophical attempts to unravel the problem of evil come under Barth's ban as he systematically applies here as elsewhere his program of the priority of revelation over all human philosophy. But the interpreter of Barth cannot stop here, as Madden and Hare did, as if Barth had said his final word on the problem of evil.

In *Church Dogmatics* III/1 ("Creation As Justification"), Barth states that Genesis 1:31 (the world is good) is a Christological assertion and must be understood in terms of Christ. Barth's total theological

---

4. Ibid., pp. 147, 159.
5. Springfield, Ill.: Charles C. Thomas, 1968.

method is complicated so a short excursus on an aspect of this methodology is necessary to explain his Christological understanding of Genesis 1:31.

Historically, Roman Catholic and Protestant theologians have affirmed that God created the universe and man for man to enjoy life in God's creation and fellowship with God. The entrance of sin destroyed this arrangement (covenant) of creation. So God must now do a new thing. He must introduce redemption into his world to save it for its original purposes. This is the second covenant of grace or redemption. Barth does not accept this traditional structure of covenants. To him there is only one covenant: the covenant of his love and redemption in Jesus Christ. All Old Testament covenants are diverse expressions of this one covenant of redemption. If this is the case, then creation is part of the covenant of redemption. For this reason Barth can take Genesis 1:31— God's pronouncement that creation is good—Christologically. When God said that, he had his eye on the cross and resurrection of Christ.

Evil does call into question the goodness and love of God. The Christian theologian does not resort to any traditional philosophical answer or to any kind of clever scheme like that of Leibniz. I doubt if Barth ever knew that such a book as Anderson's existed, but he reproduces the same answer. The cross is the clearest revelation of God's love, goodness, and wisdom. Therefore, when tragedy in any of its forms, from the mildest to the most shocking incidents, happens, the Christian finds his comfort by looking once again to the cross of Christ where there is no shadow present but only the bright light of divine truth that tells us of the unspeakable love of God. The distressed Christian (and the Christian can suffer as much distress in tragedy as the unbeliever) looks to the cross and is there reassured that no matter how brutal or cruel the tragedy, the love of God shines brighter and stronger than the doubts and uncertainties born of tragedy.

In fact, Barth says that Leibniz inadvertently expresses this same idea. In a statement out of line with his rationalistic scheme, Leibniz states that the real answer to the problem of evil is to be found in Christ. Christologically understood, this is the best of all possible worlds. The world is good (Gen. 1:31) with an eye to Christ. The best of all possible worlds that God chose was that world in which Christ is the Member and Head of creation, in which Christ is the Lord, Hope, and Savior of man, in which Christ as the God-man, perfect in each nature, is the perfection of God, the perfection of the universe, and the perfection of the ways of God.

At this point Anderson and Barth affirm the same thing. There are no rational explanations of the irrationality of evil. There is no philosophy which turns pessimism into optimism. But there is the cross. And that cross gives the Christian the ability and strength to tolerate evil, to live with confusion, to endure ambiguity, and to suffer through great evils. No event of evil can be so terrible that it can undermine the love of God as revealed at the cross. The bleeding wounds of Christ are more powerful to comfort than the bleeding wounds of evil are able to create doubt or distrust.

Section 24: Evil and the Doxological Verdict

In the last chapter of his work *The Providence of God*, G. C. Berkouwer discusses theodicy. Berkouwer, in the line of Dutch Reformed and Calvinistic scholarship, takes the solution which he thinks is truest to the Reformed and biblical position. He appreciates Barth's solution but does not believe that it is the completely biblical one, as novel and helpful as it is.[6]

Berkouwer is also as testy as Barth is against any kind of philosophical or religious resolution of the problem of evil. The Christian attitude is to be found in Scripture and nowhere else. But what does Scripture say about evil?

Scripture does not engage in long discussions on how a good God can coexist with, or tolerate, evil. Rather Scripture says over and over again, particularly in the psalms, that God is Victor. The devil is not out of hand. Evil is not running loose unchecked. Sinful men do not do all that they please. God's hands are not tied nor is God finite. God is Lord, Master, and Sovereign. He will triumph over all the evils of the world. God has revealed this; it is stated clearly in Holy Scripture. It is not a matter of reason, philosophy, speculation, or hope burning eternal in the human breast. It is a matter of divine revelation.

The response of the Christian is then that of praise; it is doxological. God has ruled, does rule, and will rule. His purposes will not be thwarted. His triumph is assured. God, not evil, has the final word. And therefore Christian man breaks into song in honor, gratitude, and praise to the God who is his Victor. And so Berkouwer ends his discussion by saying: " 'God is enthroned upon the praises of Israel.' This is the beginning and the end of true theodicy."[7]

6. Gerrit C. Berkouwer, *Studies in Dogmatics*, vol. 2, *The Providence of God* (Grand Rapids: Eerdmans, 1952).
7. Ibid., p. 294.

Section 25: The Eschatological Verdict

To some theologians there is no answer in this life to the problem of evil. Evil is irrational and enigmatic. It cannot be illuminated or alleviated by philosophical or theological explanations. Yet these theologians believe that God is good, loving, holy, and wise.

Both the learned and the unlearned have said that we make our heaven and hell now, on this earth. Kant, the greatest of the modern philosophers, thought this idea was the purest expression of superficiality. Many evil men live good lives in the sense that they suffer from no diseases, no adversities torture them, and no poverty blights them. Many good men live wretched lives. They may be ill or sickly, never experiencing good health; adversity in one of its many forms may subject them to years of painful, heartbreaking existence; or they may be persecuted and martyred for their faith.

Kant contended that when men die, the good and the evil, the books of morality and goodness are out of balance. Only in a world to come can the wicked receive what they ought to receive for their wickedness and the good receive the reward for their sufferings and injustices. In theological language, Kant's theodicy was eschatological.

Some Christian theologians see the matter the same way Kant did. No present theodicy is really satisfactory. Our knowledge in this world is not such that we can resolve the problem of evil. The resolution can only come in the next world. Only then can we actually see God is good, loving, and wise regardless of the amount of evil that men have suffered. In that this is a resolution of the problem in another world, it is called the eschatological verdict. The Christian has the fortitude to endure evil because he has the *hope* of this final, eschatological vindication of God.

BIBLIOGRAPHY

The newer discussions about evil being the most difficult of all problems of Christian faith or as the refutation of any belief in God will be found in the following representative works.

Farrer, A. *Love Almighty and Ills Unlimited.* London: Collins, 1962.
Hick, J. *Evil and the Love of God.* New York: Harper & Row, 1966. A comprehensive historical survey as well as containing Hick's own resolution of the problem.
Religious Studies. April 1969. Essays by Bowker, Richman, and Wainwright.

IX
Biblical Materials

Section 26: Job

The Book of Job is generally recognized as the unique book of Holy Scripture which deals with suffering and the underlying problem of evil. The interpretation and meaning of this book are not as obvious as previous generations of expositors have thought. Our sole concern will be to note four themes in the Book of Job that provide biblical perspective on the issues of suffering and evil.

The real meaning of the book is that Job loves God for the sake of the being, perfection, goodness, and justice of God and not for any particular earthly blessing or benefit. Satan says "Does Job fear God for nought?" (Job 1:9, RSV). Or as the Jerusalem Bible phrases it, "Job is not God-fearing for nothing, is he?" The implication is that Job's piety is based on his prosperity, and if he is given a solid sock of evil, his piety will vanish. The whole situation is a mystery to Job, but God proves to Satan that people who trust God and love him do so for what he is, and therefore evil does not destroy their faith.

Jonathan Edwards's great work *A Treatise on Religious Affections* parallels this idea. Edwards tries to differentiate between the real Christian experience and mere psychological religious fireworks. For example, some people saw huge texts of Scriptures in the skies in golden letters. Edwards's thesis was that real conversion and real faith were not to be found in any kind of unusual psychological experience or vision. Faith was loving God for what he was in himself and for the pure benefits

136

of the gospel. The theses of Job and of Edwards then come to the same point: real faith is not for reward but for God himself, and therefore (in the case of Job) evil does not eventually disturb Job because his faith is not in some earthly goodness which evil can destroy.

Another theme in Job is an eschatological one. "For I know that my redeemer liveth, and that he shall stand at the latter day upon the earth: And though after my skin worms destroy this body, yet in my flesh shall I see God: Whom I shall see for myself, and mine eyes shall behold, and not another; though my reins be consumed within me" (Job 19:25–27).

The note in the *Oxford Annotated Bible* is ambiguous suggesting that maybe Job will have his Vindicator (who need not be God) in this life, or maybe in the next life, but the real point is that "the vision of God will be sufficient" for resolving his problem. The eschatological solution is not ruled out but made a less likely interpretation. The *Jerusalem Bible*'s note is rather cagily written so as not to counter too sharply recent critical scholarship that challenges the traditional (and Latin Vulgate) understanding, yet does look for the final vindication of Job in the bodily resurrection.

From the standpoint of textual problems, we can indicate three possible interpretations:

(1) At the minimum the text says that somehow, sometime in the future, Job will be vindicated. His case, written with an iron stylus with lead for ink and rock for a writing surface (Job 19:24), will endure through the ages until some man comes along, reads it, and declares that Job is vindicated in spite of the arguments of his friends.

(2) In the world to come, after the flesh of Job has perished, Job shall yet see God who will vindicate Job.

(3) The traditional interpretation is that after his bodily resurrection, with his own body and his own eyes, Job will see God and with his own ears hear his vindication by God.

The message, no matter the interpretation, is that some evil is not punishment. A man is not afflicted necessarily because of something he has done. And therefore God will not desert him. Such a man will be vindicated. The problem with the text is the when and the where. But the suffering man may take courage and bear his suffering and his encounter with evil in the hope of future vindication.

In Job 38–41, God sets forth many instances of natural phenomena and asks if Job understands them. Job does not. Job is asked about his understanding of God's creation in which Job lives and participates and in which he is in immediate association. He eats, lives, breathes, and survives in the midst of God's creation and providence. In spite of the immediacy of his contact with creation, Job is at a loss to explain it all.

If Job cannot comprehend the creation in which he lives, how can he ever hope to comprehend the secret providences of God? If he flubs his test about the creation that surrounds him, he must then be infinitely confused about the overarching providence of God whereby God controls and cares for the moral, spiritual, and eternal concerns of man.

But Job does trust God in creation. He does rely upon the seasons and the cycles of nature. And if Job can trust God in creation, why can he not trust God in providence? Job's attitude should then be as follows: if he can trust God in creation and in the ordinary course of providence, he must then also trust God in the higher providences, in the secret counsels to which he is not privy. The problem of evil is not solved for Job, but Job learns how to live with it. He learns that he may well trust God in the mysteries of evil, for he has learned to trust God and his goodness and wisdom in the clarities of creation.

There is also an instrumental aspect to Job's discussion of evil. "And the Lord restored the fortunes of Job, when he had prayed for his friends; and the Lord gave Job twice as much as he had before. . . . And the Lord blessed the latter days of Job more than his beginning; and he had fourteen thousand sheep, six thousand camels, a thousand yoke of oxen, and a thousand she-asses. He had also seven sons and three daughters. . . . And in all the land there were no women so fair as Job's daughters; and their father gave them inheritance among their brothers. And after this Job lived a hundred and forty years, and saw his sons, and his sons' sons, four generations. And Job died, an old man, and full of days" (Job 42:10–17, RSV).

There are critics who as a matter of course look on this epilogue more as a sugar stick solution or fairy story ending than a real part of the solution to the mystery of the suffering of a good man. However, two matters are important for the proper understanding of this ending. These are blessings in terms of Job's culture. The record surely does not mean that all this came to pass at once. The picture here is not so much that of the private fortune of a single man but the accumulation of a vast estate of a typical sheik of the Middle East. Apparently the kind of evils that a man of a great estate was prone to suffer were matched by the kinds of good things that may come his way.

But the more important matter is that Job's sufferings, his patience, his refusal to curse God and die, and his repentance and humiliation (42:1–6) do result instrumentally in a greater prosperity, a concept which occurs in the New Testament in a more exalted and eschatological motif (Rom. 8:18 ff.). Even the Greek text suggests that the ending of Job portends the higher resolution of Romans 8:18, for it suggests the final blessedness of Job in the resurrection ("It is written, that he will rise again with those whom the Lord will raise up," Septuagint). As it happens in the New Testament so it happens here that in attempting some resolution of the problem of evil the instrumental perspective and the eschatological perspective overlap.

Section 27: Psalms

A number of psalms contain complaints or gripes to God. God ought to act as a God of justice, love, and equity; but world events seem to indicate just the opposite. This appears contradictory to the psalmist and gives him the blues. When the evil man prospers and the good man suffers, the piety of the good man seems a mockery. This leads to spiritual confusion. In these psalms we see the man of the Old Testament bump head-on into the problem of evil within the four walls of his own village. It is part of his daily fare of living.

In Psalm 73 the man of God reflects over the apparent discrepancy between the way the world ought to go if God is the ruler and the way it is actually going. The prosperity of the wicked has confused the psalmist. He has almost stumbled and nearly slipped—figurative images of moral responses. In verses 4 through 11 he vividly pictures the different kinds of prosperity of wicked people and their seeming exemption from any judgment of God. "And they say, 'How can God know? Is there knowledge in the Most High?'" (Ps. 73:11, RSV).

In contrast to this is the uselessness of the psalmist's spiritual life (vv. 13–16). Regardless of his personal piety, he is stricken and smitten in spiritual confusion and perplexed about what he shall tell his children concerning the value of spiritual exercises.

The change comes in verse 17. It is a change in perspective. He went into the sanctuary of God and saw the matter as it ought to be seen.

The idea is not that he went to a special place—the Temple or some part of it. But he went to the Temple where he heard the recitation of the Word of God in the liturgy or readings or chants. In the sanctuary, hearing by whatever means the Word of God, he saw the situation from the perspective of divine revelation.

The psalmist is very honest. His soul had become embittered, and he had been pricked in heart (v. 21) when he saw the advantages of the wicked. But he admits that he felt this way when he had the matter out of focus. He did think stupidly and ignorantly, and his powers of reflection were not much better than an animal's (v. 22). Such honesty is to be commended for it shows the ability of the psalmist to voice his problems to God. Throughout Protestantism such spiritual honesty and moral integrity have been unfortunately replaced by an unrealistic and saccharine piety which is untrue to life.

In the light of the Torah, the Law, the Revelation, the psalmist sees matters as they are. The ungodly are under the wrath of God. Their great prosperity and security is apparent but not real. Judgment will eventually overtake them (vv. 17–20). God may seem to be asleep now and in a dream (that is, God doesn't seem to be on the job as moral adjudicator of human life; compare similar language in 1 Kings 18:27); but God is going to wake up. And when he does, watch out.

The reverse is also true. The bad lot of the righteous is really not a bad lot. God is really with the righteous, and the piety of the righteous will be rewarded. It is worth it to trust God.

The problem of evil in the practical experience of the psalmist is regarded in two interlocking directions. First, the psalmist regains his perspective. He had let things get out of focus. Wicked generals, corrupt kings, wicked businessmen, pirating professional men, career criminals, clever gangsters, men trafficking in human flesh seem to go unchecked and with impunity toward the law. God seems to have no leash on them. Yet this is all a loss of perspective. When perspective is regained, all appears right again. These men are seen for what they are, and their awful destiny is declared.

This perspective is gained from the sanctuary, from the place where the Word of God is heard. So it is divine revelation which restores the perspective. It is divine revelation that says that evil does have its end, its final day in court under the wrath of God. And divine revelation says that the righteous man does have as his greatest possession God himself —"Whom have I in heaven but thee" (v. 25).

And so the original distress of the psalmist over the concrete experience of evil as he saw it in Israel is dissipated when through divine revelation he does see that God is Moral Adjudicator, Moral Vindicator, still Lord of men's conscience and acts, and final Disposer of the destinies of the evil and the righteous.

Section 28: Habakkuk

Habakkuk has been called the Job of the Minor Prophets. Perhaps there are no stouter words addressed to God in Holy Scripture than in this book. It also stands in marked contrast to superficial piety. To some especially pietistic people, strong words addressed to God are blasphemous or impious or show unholy unbelief. This is but another case where divine revelation and mistaken notions of the content of divine revelation clash.

Habakkuk complains directly and sharply to God. God is not keeping moral house in Israel (1:2–4). The law is slack, justice is never obtained, the wicked take advantage of the righteous, and whatever law there is, is perverted. If God is moral, just, holy, and fair, how can these conditions prevail in Israel? Here again the problem of evil crops up in day-by-day experience in village life in Israel.

God answers Habakkuk by saying that God will punish the wicked in Israel (1:5–11). The Chaldeans are a fierce and cruel people who will come to Israel as God's avengers. Judgment will come. God's moral concern is not lax. Evil will get its due and will get it hard and tough!

But to Habakkuk this complicates the problem. In some ways the Chaldeans are more evil than the Israelites. The Chaldeans are incredibly cruel (1:14–17).

This is all out of harmony with the nature of God. God is the Holy One (1:12); his eyes are too holy to look on evil with any pleasure; and he is a Rock who is set for the chastisement of men.

Habakkuk then faces right up to God and says, "Why dost thou look on faithless men, and art silent when the wicked swallows up the man more righteous than he?" (1:13, RSV). The Jerusalem Bible is even more direct: "Why do you look on while men are treacherous, and stay silent while the evil man swallows a better man than he?"

Habakkuk knows that he has spoken forthrightly and stoutly. He now prepares himself for God's answer. What is God going to say about the problem of evil as it now relates to the cruel Chaldeans (in 2:1, notice the expression *my complaint*)?

God says he will answer Habakkuk. It will be in the form of a vision, that is, a divine revelation. Further, it will be a clear vision—"to be easily read" (JB). But it is not going to come immediately. When God decides to give his revelation, he will give it. Nothing can delay it.

This means that there is a gap between the time the prophet takes his stance on the tower (2:1) and when God gives the vision, the answer, the revelation. In this period, this gap, this delay, God's moral integrity will be under a cloud. The unregenerate man ("he whose soul is not upright within him," v. 4) cannot endure this cloud. He will call God's moral integrity into question. He will not believe that God is not mocked.

But the regenerate man ("the righteous") shall live by faith. That is, in the gap, in the interval, he will trust God's moral integrity. He will believe in God's judgments. The moral confusion is only apparent. The delay of God is not an endless postponement. So between the day of the complaint and the final vision the man who really believes in God, who is righteous, lives in faith that God will in his time answer the problem of evil as concretely raised by the wicked career of the Chaldean nation.

The answer here is eschatological. There is no immediate or now answer to the question of evil. The vision is yet future. Faith can live with the ambiguity of evil because it knows there is inevitable, infallible, eschatological resolution.

The author of Hebrews uses this text in a similar way (Heb. 10:32–39). His problem is the suffering of the Christians. These Christians had "endured a hard struggle with sufferings, sometimes being publicly exposed to abuse and affliction, . . . and you joyfully accepted the plundering of your property" (Heb. 10:32–34, RSV). But God has promised. There is an eschatological word. The suffering Christian will get what God has promised, but a promise is something future, something eschatological. At this point the author of Hebrews gives Habakkuk an added interpretation. It is not the vision that comes as the answer, it is the Coming One—Jesus Christ (Heb. 10:37).

Here the resolution to evil is both eschatological and Christological. The coming Lord of the Christian will avenge and reward the faithful Christian. The evil workers, the persecutors, the ones cruel to God's dear children will receive their just punishment. "My righteous one shall live by faith" but if a man doubts God's final verdict on good and evil "my soul has no pleasure in him" (Heb. 10:38, RSV).

In this connection faith is believing during that interval in which God does seem to be silent, when the righteous are cruelly treated, and when the wicked seem to be hemmed in by no walls that God will resolve the problem of evil. Faith is this human response to the eschatological-Christological resolution of the problem of evil.

Section 29: Luke 13:1–5

Our Lord refers to an incident in which Galileans were offering sacrifices and the soldiers of Pilate came upon them and slaughtered them so that the blood of the sacrificial animals and their human blood flowed together. He refers to a second instance in which in the construction of a tower in Siloam, or in the collapse of the structure, eighteen people were killed. Although at the present time there is no particular historical information on these two events, this does not change what our Lord was saying.

His point is that particular tragedies are not necessarily the result of particular sins. They may be. The dope addict who dies of an overdose and the drunkard who kills himself in an auto accident experience a direct tragedy from their sinful deeds. But this is not universally true. It is therefore not fair (because not uniformly the case) to charge a person with personal sin when he experiences some specific tragedy.

Leibniz emphasized this point centuries later when he stated that natural evils are the outcome of moral evils. The sin of man brings the curse of God. So tragic things in general happen to people in general because people are sinners.

However, our Lord does warn that man's specific sin will eventually bring specific judgment if there is no specific repentance. Nevertheless, there is no necessary connection between tragic experiences and personal sins but tragedies in general because we are sinners in general (more on this later).

Section 30: Romans 8:18–25

This passage presents a particular difficulty. It is a compact passage, replete with difficult expressions, and of immense theological importance for the problem of evil. A cursory summary must suffice.

The problem of evil takes on the specific form of "the sufferings of this present time." These sufferings are the result of man's sin and apostasy from God putting him under the "bondage to decay." This decay is in contradiction to the divine purpose (*telos*) of God in creation. But under this judgment of God the creation is subjected to frustration of its original *telos*, the creation groans, and the Christian groans. On top of all of these the bondage to decay has created a fundamental weakness in man (v. 26).

But this evil existence is not the end of God's purposes for the creation of man. When man sinned and became subject to the bondage of decay, God initiated a hope (v. 20). There is to be a freedom, a glorious liberty of the children of God, an adoption of the sons of God which is the resurrection of their bodies.

All of these things are "the glory that is to be revealed to us" (v. 18).

The theodicy of this passage is obviously eschatological. Our present experience is one of suffering, decay, weakness, and death. There is no rationalization for it. There is no optimizing the present situation. The only thing instrumental is the encouragement of hope of things yet to come. But the resolution is future and therefore eschatological. The present evil will be overwhelmed in the presence of the future glory. The problem of evil is not explained or rationalized, but the Christian is guided in how to tolerate it, and to hope for its resolution and so endure it, and rest assured that with God there is the victory and in that victory the resolution of the enigma.

Section 31: 2 Corinthians 4:16–18

This passage is similar to Romans 8:18 ff. Evil appears as the wasting away of the outer nature. This means that man in his body is subject to disease, corruption, and finally death. This wasting away is called further a "slight momentary affliction." It is also identified with "the things that are seen."

Paul then sets up a diametrically opposite parallel. In place of the wasting outer nature is the ever-renewed inner man, the true man, the real spiritual self. The present affliction will be replaced by "an eternal weight of glory beyond all comparison." And this is the realm of the unseen and therefore eternal. (This is perhaps the most Platonic passage in the whole New Testament.)

Here again is the blending of the instrumental and the eschatological. Our present experiences of evil do prepare us for future glory and are so instrumental. But this glory is not now but future and therefore eschatological. Again the motif is not the rationalization of evil through an intellectualistic theodicy, but the promises of divine revelation which enable Christians to have some understanding of the nature of their adverse experiences and what will be the final glorious outcome of them. Knowing this they can adjust better to the ambiguities of the evils they suffer in their bodies as they outwardly perish under the assault of a possible range of thousands of diseases.

Section 32: The Book of Revelation

A subtitle for the Book of Revelation could well be "A Handbook for Martyrs." The basic purpose of the book is to encourage the persecuted

Christians and persecuted churches in the last decades of the first Christian century.

Certainly the problem of evil bears down here as hard as it does in the entire Scripture when one reads of the terrible things done to Christians. Beasts, monsters, plagues, butcheries, and rivers of blood parade across the pages of the Book of Revelation. The paradox of the Book of Revelation is the contrast of pictures of rivers of blood and the triumphs of God. The contest of good and evil, God and the devil, saint and persecutor, angels and demons comes out in the fullest revelation and manifestation more than in any other part of all of Holy Scripture. This is the end drama. Here the final word must be said. And what is that final word?

Every evil person will receive his proper reward and be assigned to his proper place.

Every wicked deed will receive its just and reasonable judgment.

Every persecuted saint will receive a compensation far in excess of his suffering.

Every righteous act will receive its proper reward, and every righteous person will be assigned his rightful place.

Hell is the end of all that is evil, wicked, sinful, immoral, unbelief, and anti-God.

Heaven, really the new Jerusalem, is the place of complete felicity, and bliss, and contentment.

All that is started in Genesis comes to its rightful, just, and proper conclusion in the Book of Revelation.

The Book of Revelation bunches together all of the biblical motifs on either the resolution or the perspectives of toleration for the problem of evil, such as:

God is the final Victor in all that he intends, both for good and for evil.

Christ is the Lamb of God and the triumphant Lion of Judah who goes from the cross with the rod of iron with which he crushes and rules his opposition.

The resolution is instrumental in that all events, good and evil, eventually do redound to the glory of the living God.

The resolution is eschatological in that all human sin and suffering, agony and death, blood and tears, are erased in the New Jerusalem and remembered no more. To the contrary, righteousness, peace, and joy reign forever and ever.

Finally, whatever the mystery of evil is, whatever its human or Satanic origin is, whatever ill and harm it may have done, its career is now over.

Whatever doubt about the goodness or wisdom or love of God is now passed. God stands in the absolute clarity as the final Victor; his love and goodness and holiness and wisdom stand under a shadow no longer. God is above all, through all, and in all, and, therefore, the final, ultimate *yes* to the goodness of creation in general and man's existence in particular.

X
Concluding Observations on the Problem of Evil

Section 33: The Critique of Optimism

Leibniz is generally considered the apostle of optimism with regard to the problem of evil. Evil is not really the terrible thing it appears to be. This is all on the surface. Beneath evil is all-pervasive good. So rather than losing heart or faith, or yielding to cynicism and bitterness, the Christian ought to rejoice that all things do work together for good.

Leibniz is also the apostle of rationalism. He can make evil look like good. He can set up a rational schema or plan or system in which evil loses its bite, its sting, its agony, and appears as part of the great universal scheme of things to promote the goodness and glory of God.

It is to be expected that such optimism and such rationalism should come in for some very substantial criticism. In that Leibniz represents a kind of mentality toward the problem of evil, attitudes and mind-sets still with us, still heard from the pulpit, still set down in print in article or book, still rehashed at funerals (of particularly tragic victims), it would be well to summarize some of these criticisms.

The first and most devastating criticism came from Voltaire, the French deist and philosopher (1694–1778). The word *philosopher* had a special usage at this time in France. It did not refer primarily to the professional or career philosopher but to those educated and sophisticated Frenchmen who were bringing the whole Western moral and spiritual tradition under withering criticism. In 1759 Voltaire published *Candide*, a ruthless, scathing, humorous attack on Leibniz's position. All the cleverness of Voltaire's satire is brought to bear to humiliate Leibniz. The basic intention is to set forth a whole series of incidents, fictional of course, in which to make the pronouncement *this is the best possible of worlds* funny and ridiculous. *Candide* is a classic on the subject of theodicy.

Whether Voltaire really felt the keenness of human suffering or whether he could not resist the temptation to show what a perfect fool Leibniz really was is debatable. The better evaluation seems to be that although Voltaire clearly saw the logical defects and odd implications of Leibniz's theory, it was really Leibniz whose heart bled for the race and not Voltaire's.

A second criticism is that Leibniz is trying to give a rational explanation of the irrational, a sane account of the insane, a reasonable justification of the surd. He therefore attempts what by the very nature of the case is impossible.

Perhaps Barth's wordy and obscure discussion of Nothingness is a good illustration of this fact. To the ordinary person *nothing* or *nothingness* means total absence, a vacuum. But some philosophers have considered it a fundamental concept of philosophy with varying interpretations. Nothingness may mean "the unformed," "the primeval stuff of the universe awaiting form," "the evil as that which negates," "the limiting edge of being." Hence, it is beyond rational explanation.

Barth attempts to describe what is beyond description, to draw a circle around that which defies all boundaries, to give an indirect rational analysis of what is essentially irrational. But the point is clear and is against Leibniz: there are no theological or philosophical rationalizations of evil.

If God can create a universe only under the conditions of compossibility which must admit the presence of evil, why should he create at all? Would it not make more sense to have no universe than have one in which there is such evil, pain, and suffering?

Leibniz works too philosophically, too much from the standpoint of natural reason, and not from a stance within revelation. Whatever his theodicy may be, it is not a Christian one (except for the remark made previously in which it was shown that Barth caught Leibniz deviating from his philosophical exposition and resorting to a Christological theodicy).

How do struggle for good and combat against evil make any sense if this is the best possible world? How does one improve on perfection? If what is, is right, would not efforts to change it actually make

this a world of lesser good? Yet who can deny that strong men, coura-
geous men, daring men have through science, medicine, and enlightened
legislation eliminated much suffering and social evil?

What kind of pastoral comfort can really be given? If the level of
good is a cosmic level, and not a matter of personal experience, what
does the concerned pastor say to the suffering Christian? What comfort
is it to know that the agony of one's cancer or the tragic loss of one's
dear child is pumping up the level of cosmic good?

Leibniz's theory is too instrumental. It suffers from the basic defect
of all instrumental theories. Somehow the wickedness of men, the bru-
tality of torture, the suffering of horrible diseases, and the terrible
injustices of society become relativized and all the horror, suffering,
and tragedy is declared to be more appearance than reality.

One characteristic of human existence is hope, the anticipation that
things will be better. Hope is a fundamental ingredient in Christianity
(see Jürgen Moltmann, *The Theology of Hope*). But if this is now the
best possible world, what happens to Christian hope? If time is a joy,
why long for eternity? If this is the best there is, why is there such a
thing as a scheme of divine redemption?

The preceding paragraphs summarize the types of criticisms leveled
at Leibniz. They are not necessarily fatal to his position, and it is not
likely that Leibniz would be mute if confronted by them. The purpose,
however, of presenting these criticisms is to show the kinds of problems
a person must face if he presents a theodicy essentially rationalistic and
optimistic in its fundamental structure.

Section 34: Evil and the Resurrection

It has been asserted that the principle refutation of Christianity in
recent theology comes from the problem of evil. It is declared that the
assertion that God is good, wise, and loving and the obvious data of
irrational suffering are contradictory. The data of suffering are incontrovertible. The existence of God is laden with logical problems. Philosophers may now say that not only are the theistic proofs inconclusive but
the existence of evil is a positive refutation of the existence of God.

When the automobile was invented and became popular, scientists
claimed that the human frame would shake to pieces if this new machine
went fifteen miles an hour. When fifteen miles an hour was reached, it
was asserted that there was a miscalculation and that man would disinte-

grate at twenty-five miles an hour. In space-flight man has traveled at a rate of twenty-four thousand miles an hour without degenerating into dust. Space-flight data show that however logically airtight the reasons of the earlier scientists were, the brute fact that man has survived speeds of tens of thousands of miles an hour cannot be challenged.

If Christ be risen from the dead, what happens to objections to Christian belief based on the problem of evil? Granted, the question is somewhat academic. We don't have the same kind of evidence for the bodily resurrection of Christ that we have for the speed of the Apollo space craft. But some very distinguished scholars such as Barth, Brunner, Künneth, Moltmann, Berkouwer, and Pannenberg today believe in the bodily resurrection of Christ. They maintain this position in the twentieth century regardless of certain critical problems concerning the reports, regardless of what biologists say about the character of physical death.

If the resurrection of Christ proves itself historically (as we think it does in 1 Cor. 15:1–7), then whatever is said against the existence of God from considerations of the problem of evil simply has to be wrong.

This is but to say in a very specific way something that can be said in a more general way. Christian faith is not just faith in God. Christian faith is a whole system. It involves doctrines of revelation, divine inspiration of Scripture, God's action in history, a scheme of Christian theology, and the whole rich range of Christian experience from the original act of salvation to the final end-drama. Christian faith involves the special history of Israel, of Jesus Christ, and of the Christian church. One loose bolt doesn't collapse the machine. Granted this is an understatement, but if Christianity is to be refuted, it has to be refuted in the totality of its structure. Severe trouble at one point in a system may bring the system down, but not necessarily. A serious problem within the Christian faith may weaken its total strength, but it does not mean the destruction of the Christian system.

If the bodily resurrection of Christ be proved to rest on substantial historical data, then the problem of evil may create an internal perplexity in Christian theology, but it does not bring down the Christian system.

Christian philosophers have turned the problem around (and unfortunately this has not been brought out in recent discussions on evil as being the refutation of the existence of God). In short, if evil is a problem for those who believe in God, good is a problem for those who do not believe in God. It may be outlined thusly:

The world is a complex of closed, self-contained systems (physical, chemical, biological).

Man experiences the good, an indefinable ultimate and very real.

As such this good cannot be deduced from, nor is it the product of, any of these self-contained systems.

Whatever we call it, there is a source of good beyond all the self-contained systems of the universe.

Therefore, that the world as a system of self-contained systems is not the totality of reality, for one more reality must be added, namely, the source of the good.

Section 35: Guidelines for Christian Living and the Problem of Evil

We may look at the problem of evil from two perspectives. (1) Christians may listen to the conversations of past and present theologians and philosophers in which issues and the alternatives are stated as well as the problems that attend each alternative. The treatment may be purely philosophical or purely theological or some combination of the two. The idea is to get to the root of the problem of evil and see what can be said of it in a theoretical way. The importance of this approach cannot be overstated. Without this kind of investigation, Christian theology and Christian preaching are impoverished and can become superficial and misleading. (2) One must view the problem of evil from the standpoint of pastoral concern, correctly stated by Berkouwer.

With respect to his own experience and the experiences of his fellows, the Christian must come to terms with the problem of evil. He must learn to live with the problem of evil in its concrete manifestations. The pastoral concern is not so much to set out the proposed resolution of the problem but to help Christians who suffer evil learn how to look at it and live with it. Practically speaking, the task of pastoral concern involves learning to live with the ambiguities of life, the enigmas of life, the uncertainties of life, and the problems of life in face of the fact that no theory of evil has yet been propounded in the Christian church to the satisfaction of all theologians.

The context in which a Christian thinks of the problem of evil is Holy Scripture, and the perspective for Christian understanding of pain and suffering must come from revelation.

The only God the Christian can talk about is the God of Holy Scripture. The only man Christian faith really knows is man as the creation of God. The only real historical insights Christians have are biblical. The only realistic definitions of evil, sin, and Satan, or, of love, pity, and justice, are definitions from Holy Scripture.

The Christian therefore cannot talk about theodicy from the terms given to him or defined for him by philosophy. This does not mean that he ignores philosophy. As a Christian theologian, he is responsible for man's thoughts outside the canon of revelation as well as those inside it. Further, there is much he can learn from the history of the problem of evil in philosophy. But in working out his own basic theology, he starts within the circle of divine revelation and works from there out, and in turn comes back to Scripture to test where his speculations have brought him.

The Christian knows that there is no explanation of evil in the precise sense in which a scientist explains a theory. To think about the problem of evil, to wrestle with the issue of theodicy theoretically, theologically, and personally is a confession of honesty. It is the willingness to face ambiguity, complexity, shadows, enigmas, and darkness as a Christian. It is the willingness to bring his faith into testing without pious glosses or trite solutions. The aim of theodicy is not to show that the Christian can untie a knot that a philosopher cannot or that the Christian faith is superior to all other religions in understanding evil.

There is only one way to approach the question of evil and suffering, and that is through humility. Nevertheless, in the effort to gain all insights possible from whatever source, the Christian must insist that at least one foot be kept in the circle of divine revelation. If the problem is approached with this openness, this freedom, this humility, then Christians can learn to live with the raw edge of suffering and the ambiguities and torments of evil.

Not all suffering or sin or evil is proper material for theodicy. Evil may come as a just consequence of foolish, sinful, or unwise decisions and actions of men. Further, God is a God of judgment in history (Rom. 1–2) as well as at the end of time. The judgment of God upon men for their depravity is not material for theodicy. Where people are responsible for evils that occur, these evils are only remotely the concern of theodicy. Evils and tragedies that come to people, who for all intents and purposes ask for them, are not really moral problems and therefore not part of the discussion of theodicy.

Holy Scripture is not a book of Pollyanna. Scripture does not shrink from the problem of evil. A portion of the biblical evidence for this has been reviewed. Scripture does not dull the sharp edge of tragedy or the cruel force of evil. Nor does it simplify the complexity, ambiguity, and turmoil of human existence. "It is man who breeds trouble for himself as surely as eagles fly to the height" (Job 5:7, JB). "Yet man is born into trouble, as the sparks fly upward" (Job 5:7). Nor does the Scripture shrink from some of the darkness of the cross calling it the weakness of God (2 Cor. 13:4).

The temptation to preach the gospel according to Pollyanna is very great in the Christian church. We are told that real faith in God excludes doubt, questions, perplexities, confusions, enigmas, and hesitations. Cries of bewilderment and despair are not appropriate in the church.

The ideal in such Christian opinion is more that of the Stoics than that of Holy Scripture. To the Christian Stoic, nothing batters the brow nor bloodies the head. All is taken as from God, and to question or complain is to doubt. The devil and depravity are at work even in Christian hearts, and this is the origin of Christian confusion and uncertainty. This may make nice preaching and be reassuring to some Christians, but this is not to be honest with the problem of evil. More importantly it is not biblical.

What can Pollyanna Christianity say about the Book of Job? If true faith is stoiclike faith, why does Holy Scripture detail the complaints of the heart of a man of God? If true faith is stoiclike faith, then why the depression psalms? And what can the Pollyanna Christian say of the cry from the cross, "My God, my God, why have you deserted me?" (Matt. 27:46, JB).

Calvin's wise dictum was that Christians must learn to live within the promises of God. God has not promised man everything. It is not unusual to hear from the pulpit, "Jesus Christ has the answer to every one of your problems." Does this mean God has promised all? What God has promised, he has promised in his Word. As Calvin said, God does not toy with us with empty words. If God has promised something, he means it. But as a matter of fact, there are a lot of things he has not promised. Calvin insists that we can bind God only to what God has promised. Therefore, to give Christians the impression, in whatever glowing, pious words, that God has promised all and everything, is wrong. It is unbiblical, for if we cannot hold a man to what he has not promised, neither can we bind God to something he has not spoken in his Word. Christians have the right to claim all that God has promised within the total understanding of the biblical revelation about the conditions of

God's promises; but they must also learn from Scripture what God has not promised. God has not promised that no babies shall die. God has not promised to spare us from dreadful diseases. God has not promised that Christians will never have accidents. God has not promised that Christians will never perish in travel—by land, sea, or air. He has not promised that we shall be spared from economic depressions and invasions of foreign armies. He has not promised to end forever storms, tornadoes, and typhoons. He has not promised that all our children will be born without physical or mental defects.

It is a hard lesson to learn, and some Christians collapse rather than learn it. But the mature Christian learns to live within the promises of God and is not thrown into confusion when something happens to him.

God is not the devil. The devil by definition is that spirit which is pure evil. He is that spirit that can only will sin, evil, hurt, harm, and wickedness. Whatever name we give him, that is his character. Therefore he can never be God.

God by definition is that Spirit which loves, which wills the good, which seeks man's benediction and beatitude. God wills the salvation of man. God desires the New Jerusalem for all men. God grieves and sorrows over tragedy, sin, and evil.

Experiences can be confusing. Tragedy can paralyze the reason. Suffering can cloud the clarity of our theological convictions. But never should the Christian let the evil, the sin, the suffering, the ambiguity of life confuse his mind between what is of Satan and what is of God—what God wills in his goodness and what Satan wills in his unspeakable depravity and wickedness.

God is a God of power. This is expressed many ways in the biblical record. God is Lord. God is Almighty. God is Sovereign. God is the Potter. God is the Director, Controller, and Fulfiller of history.

Therefore evil, sin, and the devil are never beyond God. There is a dualism in Scripture but in view of the power of God, the lordship of God, the dualism is purely a relative dualism.

The power of God in Scripture is not the same doctrine of the power of Allah in the Muslim faith. Nor is it the Absolute Power of some of the theologians of the Middle Ages. God's power, like all his attributes, is in the context of all his attributes. His power, his love, his pity, his wrath, his holiness, and his grace all live on the same street. Nonetheless, God is a God of might and power, and therefore evil is never greater than God, sin is never more powerful than God, and Satan is never beyond God's tether.

God is incomprehensible and mysterious. The problem of evil is not a problem unique from other problems in understanding God. Christian theology has been faithful to the biblical revelation in speaking of the greatness of God, the transcendence of God, the incomprehensibility of God, and the mysterious character of many of his acts and providences. There is then a limit to whatever man may think about God on whatever subject. This applies to the problem of evil, and, therefore, every discussion of this problem by Christian or non-Christian must be tempered by these considerations. God is in his heaven as Lord, and man is on the earth as servant, and a healthy measure of humility of the servant before the Lord is never out of place, whether in service or in matters of the intellect.

God can work in the area of sin. God is not a God who can work only where there is purity and holiness. God can work where there is evil, rebellion, and sin.

For example, God took the evil intentions of Joseph's brothers and Potiphar's wife and out of them worked a work of providence and saved Joseph's kin from starvation (Gen. 50:20).

God took the evil of the Jews, the cowardice of the disciples, the indifference of the masses, and the unprincipled action of Pilate and the Romans and wrought the redemption of the world in the cross of Christ (Acts 2:23).

God took the pride of Pharaoh, the might of his armies, and the prejudices of the Egyptians and manifested his power to save and redeem a group of slaves from one of the greatest military powers of that ancient millennium (Rom. 9:17).

No matter how great evil is, no matter the cunning of men, no matter the depravity of society, no matter the weakness of believers, God is not limited, his arm is not shortened, nor is his power restricted. Whenever he wills, he can enter the very center of the arena of evil and in his wisdom and power turn it to his purposes and the fulfillment of his will.

Epilogue

The range of topics that can be classified as Christian apologetics, or philosophy of religion, or philosophical theology is very great, and we have made only a modest attempt to work on the central problems of our own version of Christian apologetics.

We append here some themes or topics that may be used to enlarge or expand or supplement the use of this book as a text. These themes or topics may be subjects of lectures by the instructor, part of the reading assignment for the students, or suggestions for term papers and/or discussions.

(1) Is revelation a substitute for philosophy, or how are the two disciplines related? Choose a theologian anywhere in the history of theology, and show how he related the two disciplines.

(2) Our legal systems have developed criteria of evidence and fact. List the important ones, and evaluate their usefulness or applicability for Christian apologetics.

(3) Contemporary philosophy speaks much about verification. Is verification one set procedure or are there different kinds of verification? How do the conclusions you have reached apply to Christian apologetics?

(4) Is there anything unique about Christian revelation, or theological beliefs as such, that calls for the use of criteria of truthfulness we do not use in other disciplines? Investigate some theologian and see how he answers this question.

(5) Some theologians believe that sin so disturbs man's reasoning about God that man can think of God correctly only in a state of grace; others argue that truth is truth regardless of sin. How would Emil Brunner or John Calvin or Pelagius (or any other theologian of your choosing) answer this problem?

(6) Religion involves an experience of some special kind that mathematics or logic doesn't. Where does experience fit into theology? What verification value is there in experience? What are the logical problems

if too much weight is placed upon experience? What theologian puts a major emphasis on experience in theology and philosophy of religion?

(7) How would you differentiate and evaluate the following kinds of experiences: moral, mystical, existential, and pragmatic?

(8) Can the superiority of Christian ethical teachings and the Christian set of values over those of other religions be demonstrated? Is there an apologetic issue at stake here?

(9) One of the major debates of the twentieth century is whether a Christian and a non-Christian have common ground for discussing whether or not Christianity is true. This has important implications for Christian missions. Is there a common ground? How does your answer determine your apologetics and your strategy in evangelism and missions? What theologians have debated this issue?

(10) It is said that no man is an atheist. In his heart of hearts he believes in God; or there are no atheists in foxholes. Can a man be an honest atheist with integrity or is atheism itself a reverse form of a religious conviction?

(11) Bultmann does not set forth any kind of formal apologetic system, but he does have one. Decode from his writings how he thinks believers are convinced that they are believing a kerygma that is true.

(12) Show the indebtedness of Brunner's apologetics to the writings of Kierkegaard.

(13) Why does Barth reject apologetics? Do you really think he does, or does he introduce the apologetic issues in a different form or from a different perspective?

(14) Tertullian's attitude toward philosophy (what has Jerusalem to do with Athens?) is debatable. How do you assess this debate?

(15) There is now a revival of process philosophy due to the influence of men like Whitehead and Teilhard. Process philosophy is being used by theologians for apologetic purposes. Indicate why they have done this. How does process philosophy lead to process theology and process apologetics? Are process theologians repeating the errors of nineteenth-century liberalism and its use of philosophy, or have they managed to avoid this danger?

(16) Some of Hegel's followers thought that he had produced the final vindication of Christianity. Explain why they should think this way.

(17) Francis Schaeffer's books are very popular for their unusual apologetic thrust. How do you evaluate his efforts in comparison to other representative schools of apologetics?

(18) Dooyeweerd has made a very ambitious attempt in rewriting a

Reformed view of apologetics. Explain his system and your reactions to it.

(19) James Orr was a great apologist of a past generation. What was his basic position? How does it stand up with the present state of philosophy and theology?

(20) Van Til has written a library of his own on apologetics. Is his system unique, or is it the traditional Reformed position in apologetics in a more modern and novel form?

(21) There has been much written about the relationship of Christianity to history. What are the apologetic issues in history? Is history for or against the Christian faith? Is this an oversimplification of a complex problem?

(22) How does one's view of biblical criticism affect his apologetics? How does Barth or Brunner or Tillich or Knox relate biblical criticism to his theology?

(23) What is concessive apologetics? Where is it realistic? What is its danger?

(24) How will the future technological civilization determine our understanding of man? What problems do you anticipate an advanced technological society will create for Christian faith?

(25) Is Freud or any other theory of psychiatry for or against the Christian faith? What relationship do you see between Christian apologetics and our present psychiatric knowledge?

(26) Some theologians think that Sartre has a real contribution to make to Christian thinking. What might this be? Do you agree or disagree?

(27) Many lay people say that we do not need to rely on any kind of intellectual defense of the faith as Christian apologetics suggests but upon faith and the Holy Spirit. In what sense are they right and in what sense are they wrong?

(28) Evangelicals such as Clark, Henry, and Carnell have written works directly or indirectly apologetical in character. Attempt to summarize the essence of their positions and contrast it with some apologist who is neoorthodox or liberal in persuasion.

(29) What would you say is the principle of verification for Christian faith in the theology of Tillich?

(30) It has been said that poets and artists are the true metaphysicians. If this is true, what are the implications for Christian apologetics?

(31) Is modern physics creating more room for freedom and con-

tingency in the universe and therefore helping Christian apologetics, or is it as deterministic as ever only in terms of the newer concepts in physics?

(32) Is evolution still an important element to be treated in Christian apologetics or has it become irrelevant? What is the relationship of any theory of the origin of the universe or life or man to the biblical doctrine of creation?

(33) There are a number of Christians who are turning to the use of analytic or linguistic philosophy for the restatement of Christian theology and apologetics. How do you assess this new kind of apologetics?

(34) Do Christians have the right to be higher critics of science and scientific method?

(35) Holy Scripture was completed almost two thousand years ago. What is the specific element or the specific character of Holy Scripture that makes it relevant for our century? Discuss this using two or three contemporary theologians and their answers to this problem.

(36) Phenomenology is a very difficult philosophy to understand, but it is a modern current option in philosophy. How could it be used as the basis of a Christian apologetics?

(37) What are the apologetic elements in Niebuhr's famous work *The Nature and Destiny of Man?*

(38) Assess what Martin Luther has said against reason and for reason. Give the supportive reasons in your assessment.

(39) Why has Martin Buber's thought been so important to Christian theologians, and what apologetic service can it fulfill?

(40) Among some theologians there has been a revival of belief in the bodily resurrection of Christ. What is their basis for this revived belief? What arguments have been urged against them?

(41) What problems does a study of comparative religions present to a Christian, especially in Christian apologetics? What do you think of the truth claims of non-Christian religions?

(42) It is claimed a new day is here in every way: technology, science, logic, linguistic analysis, sophisticated theories of verification, the New Left, existentialism, etc., and that the older apologetics and Christian evidences have now lost both relevance and appeal. We need to be making a new apologetic for the mentality and cultural changes of our times. Is this really the case? Is the old completely dated? What is new in whatever is called new? How do you see this in art, movies, novels, and music? If the claim is true, how does it affect evangelism, missions,

preaching, witnessing, church work of all sorts besides apologetics? How does this change the way we understand and use Scripture if these claims of the new are true?

Also by Bernard Ramm from Word Books:

Questions About the Spirit (QP # 98108) An easy-to-read, yet in-depth discussion of the Holy Spirit and his work with relation to topics such as beauty, politics, prayer, and many more.

The Evangelical Heritage (CL # 80316) Discovers a thread of continuity for evangelicalism by tracing the "geography" of evangelical theology. Suggests that evangelicals must be students of Holy Scripture, must know the inner structure of evangelical theology, must know their cultural climate, and must rethink the manner in which God is related to the world.

The Devil, Seven Wormwoods, and God (CL # 0041-7) Bernard L. Ramm exhorts those of the evangelical faith to listen patiently and to learn from those who do not share their views but who can offer pearls of wisdom, nonetheless. Objectively, Ramm then discusses the philosophies of such heretics as Nietzsche, Sartre, Hume, Camus, and three others in demonstrating how each does have something to offer in his turbulent writings.